Gluten Intolerance

Gluten Intolerance

When wheat is the enemy

Gisèle Frenette

" Let Food Be Thy Medicine,
And Medicine Be Thy Food! "

Hippocrates (460 - 377 B.C.)

Table of Content

Introduction

This book was written to bring hope to the thousands of people coping with a difficult to diagnose health concern. This condition can disguise itself so well it will puzzle even conscientious doctors, forcing them to review their findings repeatedly, while individuals suffering from this disease try as best they can to enjoy life. Nowadays, we are acquainted with autoimmune diseases; we discuss fibromyalgia and chronic fatigue as if they were trivial viruses, allergies are causing havoc for a large percentage of the population, and now, we have celiac disease, the new kid on the block, a condition considered rare in North America until recently.

This book is the outcome of many years of research through my work in the holistic field with hundreds of clients desperately seeking a cause and solution to their ailments. Celiac disease or gluten intolerance is not discriminatory; it will strike anyone, from infancy to the adult years including the elderly. My goal in writing this book is to elucidate the mystery surrounding this disease, permitting a quick diagnosis, as healing is close at hand for everyone; all that is needed is a bit of patience and a lot of willpower.

Through this book, the reader will acquire considerable knowledge of celiac disease, giving him the possibility of a quick and accurate diagnosis without useless wandering, therefore minimising damage to his health. Chapter one will guide us through years of research on celiac disease, followed in chapter two by a description of its causes and symptoms. Chapter three will examine diagnostic methods while the next one will discuss conditions associated with the disease.

Chapters five and six will point out where gluten can be found, as well as which foods are permitted in a gluten-free diet. The subsequent chapters will give us useful hints on how to rebuild our health, both physically and psychologically, followed by heartfelt testimonials, bringing celiac's reality to light.

This book is meant to be a comforting and valuable aid, filling you with hope and optimism on your way to better health. This is the missing link I personally searched for throughout the years. It gives me great pleasure to share it with you.

CHAPTER ONE

An unknown health hazard

Despite the fact that thousands of people throughout the world suffer from it, gluten intolerance is still relatively unknown to most. This condition masquerades under multiple forms, hindering diagnosis. Of nearly epidemic proportion, its symptoms can vary from a seemingly harmless stomachache to severe complications implicating the immune system. This disease does not discriminate between ages. Awareness of this condition is the key to controlling the extent of its damage to people's general health.

What is gluten intolerance?

A long time ago, a human being's main preoccupation was to survive, making him a food provider before all else. His life depended on surrounding plants and herbs, in addition to animal hunting. About ten thousand years ago, cultivation of cereals such as wheat started. All of the sudden, the human body had to adjust to this drastic change of diet. This brings us to question whether this change was too demanding for the human digestive tract.

Gluten intolerance, also referred to as celiac disease, is a digestive condition brought on by the ingestion of gluten, which is the protein of certain grains. The inability to properly assimilate gluten can often lead to the malabsorption of certain nutrients such as vitamins, minerals, sugars, protein, and fat. It is in fact a form of reaction from the immune system, which appears in genetically predisposed individuals. We will elaborate on the causes of this disease in the following chapter.

The true origin of the disease has not yet been discovered, but we know that certain elements from the immune system such as antibodies, cytokines and lymphocytes are implicated in the process. The immune system of people suffering from celiac disease does not function as it should. It reacts to the presence of gluten by attacking the inner lining of its small intestine, in a manner very similar to the body's rejection of an organ transplant (heart, kidney). As this part of the intestine is of major importance to the absorption of nutrients essential to life, deficiencies accumulated until a proper diagnosis is established and a gluten-free diet is started.

A total avoidance of gluten is the only solution known to date to relieve the symptoms and complications arising from celiac disease, and to promote intestinal recovery. The exclusion of gluten, in all of its forms, is to be considered a lifetime plan.

Definition of gluten

Gluten is the protein portion contained in wheat, oats, rye and barley. The two major constituents of gluten are prolamines and glutenins. The prolamine in gluten is called gliadin and is responsible for celiac disease. Gliadin is the protein fraction of wheat to which the intestine reacts by developing inflammation. Glutenin on its own is inoffensive, but since it is always accompanied by gliadin in cereals, it is automatically eliminated from the diet.

Each grain contains a different amount of gliadin. This is what determines the severity of the body's reaction. For the individual who is gluten intolerant, the body's reaction will be directly proportional to the amount of gliadin ingested.

Gliadin has a low molecular weight, which gives products made with cereal grain flours their extensibility and elasticity, in other words, its ability to rise in volume. We will discuss gluten's utility some more in chapter two.

Gliadin is the specific name given to the prolamine in wheat. Other cereals toxic to gluten intolerant individuals are also constituted of prolamines of similar composition, consequently causing the same harmful reactions in the body. Secalin is the prolamine in rye, hordein, that of barley, and avenin, that of oats. All prolamines are detrimental to celiacs and forbidden in a gluten-free diet.

History throughout the years

Gluten intolerance is not a new condition, only its classification as celiac disease is recent. It may be correct to state that one of the consequences of civilization was that a small percentage of the population whom could not tolerate wheat became ill.

As far back as 250 AD, a Roman physician, by the name of Galen gave the first description of both childhood and adult celiac disease. His writings were edited and translated in 1856. They demonstrated a remarkable knowledge of celiac disease and its symptoms. He utilized the Greek word "koiliakos"[1] which originally meant "suffering from the bowels". Passing through Latin, "k" becomes "c" and "oi" becomes "oe". If we drop the Greek ending "os", we get the word coeliac that is another spelling of celiac.

In India, as early as 1500 BC, medical literature written in Sanskrit, described intestinal diseases, including what could have been celiac disease. Sanskrit is an ancient Indic language that is the classic literary language of India.

In 1669, a Dutch physician, Vincent Ketelaer described "stomatitis aphthous" in a paper on celiac disease then known as "spruw".[2]

In was in 1888, in Britain, that Samuel Gee gave his description of celiac disease and also mentioned the role of diet in its treatment. His account was considered almost prophetic, particularly his quote: "to regulate the food is the main part of treatment... The allowance of farinaceaous foods must be small... but if the patient can be cured at all, it must be by means of diet."[3]

Other physicians continued to search for a treatment for this disease, often paediatricians, probably because children responded more rapidly to dietary changes than adults. A paediatrician named Herter also wrote about this ailment in 1908. He was such an authority on the subject that the condition was often referred to as Gee-Herter's disease. In 1918, Sir Frederick Still, another renowned children's physician, drew attention to the possible link between certain intestinal diseases and the negative effect of eating bread.

Dr. Howland developed this theme further in 1921 when he recommended the exclusion of bread, cereals and potatoes from the diet of celiac children for a determined length of time. In 1924, Dr. Haas establish the success of his banana diet. In a later paper, in 1938, he noted that a minute amount of some foods containing carbohydrates would produce diarrhea even with hardly any fat in the diet. On the other hand, eating a large amount of bananas was well tolerated even when a larger amount of fat was included.

World War II (1939-1945) brought about a remarkable discovery that led to the advancement of treatment of celiac disease in children and adults alike. In 1950, the Dutch paediatrician, Professor Dicke suggested that some cereal grains were harmful to children suffering from certain intestinal symptoms. He had noticed a connection between the sickness of a specific group of children and a particular wartime situation. During this war, Holland was under German occupation. The German troops kept all the protein rich grains such as wheat, rye and barley for themselves, forcing the general population to survive on a diet consisting of potatoes and rice. Surprisingly, the sick children seemed to thrive on this diet, becoming healthier and growing better than ever. As soon as the war ended and wheat was reintroduced into the diet, they suffered a relapse and their intestinal problems returned.[4]

Charlotte Anderson and her colleagues in Birmingham confirmed this discovery when they extracted the starch and some other constituents from the wheat flour. They concluded that the "resulting gluten mass" was the culprit in celiac disease. Therefore, since 1950, the gluten-free diet has become the basic treatment for celiac disease.

It was in 1954, during a surgery on an adult celiac patient, that Dr. Paulley first described an abnormality of the lining of the small intestine.[5] This inflammatory change was later verified on several patients and confirmed as the intestinal lesion called villus atrophy. This breakthrough was of great importance and doctors, both in the United States and throughout the world, agreed that the loss of microscopic villi that usually cover the inner lining of the small intestine was the most essential feature on which to base the diagnosis of celiac disease.

At about the same time, a new diagnostic method, what we now call a biopsy, consisting of taking a tiny sample of the lining of the stomach, was optimized to reach the lining of the small bowel. This greatly contributed to the scientific study of celiac disease. In 1956, the small bowel biopsy was perfected and became the standard technique used to diagnose celiac disease. The tube utilized to do the biopsy was innovated until completely flexible and this method was soon accepted worldwide.

In 1958, it was demonstrated that celiac disease in children and adults were identical disorders. In the 1960's, dermatologists discovered a connection between dermatitis herpetiformis (a skin condition) and the small bowel atrophy associated with the celiac condition. They also noticed that these patients responded well to a gluten-free diet. In the 1980's, Michael Marsh and his colleagues, in Manchester, England, emphasized the role of the immune system in causing the intestinal damage in celiac disease.

Diverse appellations

Celiac disease has diverse appellations. It is important to recognize the different names given to the condition to ascertain whether the subject is of concern to us or not. All names refer to the same problem; the inability to tolerate gluten found in certain grains. The word "celiac" is often spelled "coeliac", and the word "disease" can be replaced by "condition", "affection" or "syndrome".

The term "gluten sensitive enteropathy" also refers to the same condition, as well as "enteropathy from gluten intolerance". The name "sprue" is well recognized, as in "celiac sprue", which was mainly used to describe celiac disease in adult patients. Let us not forget to mention reference books that quote "sprue nostras", "idiopathic steatorrhea" or "nontropical steatorrhea", which all describe the same adult condition consisting of proven gluten intolerance.

For children, medical books will also refer to "intestinal infantilism", "Herter's disease", "Gee's disease", "Gee-Herter's disease", "Heubner-Herter's disease", and "gluten induced enteropathy". For the adult, we can add "nontropical sprue" to the listing. Last but not least, the following terms are also included in the list: "malabsorption syndrome", "gluten intolerance" and "gluten sensitivity".

To facilitate the writing and reading of this book, the terms "gluten intolerance" and "celiac disease" will be used in an equal manner. However, a difference does exist between the two. "Celiac disease" describes the condition as diagnosed by a doctor, following a small bowel biopsy with a positive result. As you can see, the term "gluten intolerance" can also include these individuals, but the opposite does not apply in such a unanimous way. For many reasons, certain people do not subscribe to the intestinal biopsy, but withdrawal of all dietary gluten is sufficient to alleviate their symptoms. A return to a regular diet including gluten is followed by the recurrence of the same symptoms. We conclude that the term "gluten intolerance» also applies to these people.

Racial and genetic predominance

We know that the immune system is in part controlled by heredity, which brings us to the conclusion that genetic factors are implicated with celiac disease. It is still unknown whether a dominant or recessive gene transmits the condition. For example, in the case of identical twins, it was noted that one of the children could be diagnosed as celiac while the other was spared.

Recent studies indicate that five to ten percent of the first-degree relatives of people diagnosed with celiac disease are also victims, and some authors dare to allege to a much higher percentage. Most diagnosed individuals can identify a family member suffering from recognizable symptoms. It is not unusual to hear them mention a relative afflicted with diarrhea, or a person suffering from a complication related to celiac disease, or even a death following an intestinal cancer.

Many researchers wonder why celiac disease is not more common in the United States, considering that it is hereditary and that many Americans are from European descent where the condition is more common. As a matter of fact, in Italy, one person out of 250 suffers from the disease, and in Ireland, one in 300. It is also very present in other nationalities including Scandinavians, Arabs and Slavic people. It is seldom a problem in Asia, Africa, China and Japan, although recently, it is sometimes seen in people of African or Asian descent.

A few theories explain why celiac disease is becoming more common in a non-European population. One factor could be the recent growing popularity of wheat. Another reason may be that many cases are overlooked during disease testing. It is also likely that a certain group of people with a certain genetic baggage is less susceptible to the condition. In North America, the ratio was inferred to as being one in 4700 individuals, but following more intensive screening programs, the ratio now suggests one in 150 or more.

CHAPTER TWO

Gluten intolerance is real

The vast majority of diseases related to the digestive system develop over a long period of time. Most people believe that if they are exempt of digestive pain or discomfort, it follows that they do not suffer from a digestive disorder. Yet, in the United States, one surgery out of three is performed because of a digestive condition. One death out of ten is attributed to a digestive cause. We can well imagine that the percentages are similar in Canada. An adequate diet that responds to each individual's needs is absolutely essential for a healthy life.

The most common food allergens are milk, eggs, wheat, nuts, corn, soy and beef. During the digestive process, all of these protein foods are converted to protein by-products. We know that most food allergens are protein waste from poorly digested meat, dairy products and the protein fraction of wheat. Most bacteria and viruses threatening the human body are also protein in nature, so the body is already programmed to attack any unidentifiable protein invaders. When the food is completely digested to its adequate form of end products (proteins into amino acids), it loses its ability to cause allergies.

Gluten intolerance is not an allergy, but it is important to familiarise ourselves with the way allergies come about. Let us now see where gluten is found.

Where is gluten found?

Wheat is an ancient tradition; archaeological digs provide evidence of its existence as far back as prehistoric times. In religion, wheat appropriated itself the rank of a sacred food. In church, we share the consecrated bread and the Eucharistic wafer at communion. Even these simple religious rituals, so appeasing to the mind and soul, can cause physical suffering to the gluten intolerant individual.

Gluten is the protein portion of wheat, as well as a constituent of oats, barley, rye and triticale, a hybrid of rye and wheat. Other flours closely connected to wheat that also contain gluten are kamut, spelt and durum semolina. All of these have to be carefully avoided by celiacs.

Gluten is an additive commonly used in food manufacturing. As gluten is a good source of protein, it is utilize to increase the protein value of certain foods. At one time, bread containing extra protein was very recommended, especially for diabetics. Gluten gives both texture and volume to baked products such as bread. During baking, gluten entraps carbon dioxide and other gases, which gives structure and volume to the baked good. Celiacs have to become accustomed to products of a much different texture. Gluten-free breads tend to crumble easily. Nowadays, a large variety of gluten-free products are found in health food stores and even at the local supermarket. There is a multitude of gluten-free recipe books available. If you are blessed with a propensity for cooking, this may well be the time to put your talents to the test.

If a gluten-free diet consisted only in averting the previously mentioned grains and their flours, it could be relatively simple to understand. However, with the recent discovery of gluten's versatility by food manufacturers, gluten avoidance has become much more complicated. While we will discuss this in great details in chapter 5, here is a general list of gluten containing foods to avoid. These foods are often forgotten when we exclude gluten from the diet:
Thickening agents
Soup base
Broth
Croutons
Stuffing
Communion's host

Bacon bits
Seafood imitation
Marinades
Breading
Sauces
Pasta
Delicatessen products
Pre-basted poultry.

Oats have been the subject of an ongoing controversy. The main problem is the difficulty encountered in identifying with certainty the amino acid responsible for the immune system's reaction. We also have to differentiate and compare the chemical components of wheat and oats before we clarify this situation. While many countries in Europe allow oats in a gluten-free diet, the United States and Canada forbid it. Many studies demonstrate that the gluten in oats has a very low to almost non-existent toxicity level. However, if one is to do his own research, more studies stating practically the opposite are available.

For a lot of celiac sufferers determined to take control of their health, the risk factors are too important. Many people choose to completely avoid oats. Of course, if a short trial period with oats added to the diet causes obvious symptoms, then the answer is easy. Unfortunately, for many celiacs, the bowel does not answer so readily. Many have no digestive disturbance whatsoever, rendering a trial period an unnecessary risk bringing them no closer to resolving the dilemma. Therefore, adding oats to a gluten-free diet is a very personal decision.

Buckwheat is often wrongly considered as part of the wheat family. The English appellation including the word "wheat" in its name is misleading, as is its ancient name of "black wheat". Buckwheat does not contain gluten.

All processed foods on the market are liable to contain gluten except for items affixed with labels clearly displaying the words "gluten-free". Whether gluten has been added to the food preparation or by cross-contamination while using the same kitchenware that served to prepare gluten-containing foods, the gluten- sensitive individual is at risk. All these extra precautions make grocery shopping a very peculiar experience that may demand a bit of patience at first. Start by asking your grocer to include gluten-free items on his shelves and check out the health food stores in your area. Online ordering is also becoming very popular. Once you locate a few gluten-free essentials, grocery shopping and life will return to near normal.

What causes celiac disease?

Researchers throughout the world continue to question the cause of celiac disease. Everyone is eager to understand the in-depth mechanism of this inflammatory toxicity. While research is slowly advancing, answers are still somewhat vague.

One theory is that gluten intolerant people are born missing an intestinal enzyme meant to digest gliadin. This deficiency would explain why they cannot properly breakdown the gluten protein hence causing an accumulation of toxins in the intestinal tract. This deficiency could be either congenital or provoked by alterations from other origins, such as an infection or the presence of parasites. This enzyme insufficiency could be partial or total, therefore explaining the different levels of severity of the disease. Another theory is that gluten intolerance is in fact an immunologic defect, which would inactivate several gastrointestinal epithelial cells.

The hypothesis of an allergy to gliadin has also been mentioned. The allergy would cause an inflammation of the intestinal lining, similar to a red rash on the skin provoked by an allergic reaction. Up to now, none of these theories are proven scientifically. More time and research is needed to elucidate this mysterious disease. The exact cause of celiac disease is still unknown.

However, we now know with certainty that developing celiac disease necessitates a genetically predisposed individual from birth who is eating cereal grains containing gluten. Even if these two factors are in place, the disease can lay dormant for years, waiting for a "trigger factor" of some sort to appear and set off the disease. Once a person is exposed to gluten, the intestinal damage can develop within a few months or can wait for ten, twenty years and even longer.

As celiac disease is a genetic disorder, there is a definite family tendency to the condition. According to Dr. Joseph Murray[1] of the Mayo Clinic in the United States, familial incidence to relative of the first-degree (parents, brothers, sisters and children) is of 10%. If a person has a parent or a child diagnosed with celiac, this individual should be readily tested for the disease. Dr. Murray adds that the condition is not solely genetic. As seen in identical twins, if one suffers from celiac disease, the other has about 70% chance to suffer from it also. If the disease were completely genetic, the incidence for identical twins would be of 100%.

Trigger factors

Since celiac disease is a genetic disorder, the tendency to acquire the disease is present at birth. Dr. Murray believes that many trigger factors can be responsible for activating the disease in a genetically predisposed person.

These "trigger factors" could be:
A sudden change to a low fat diet, which usually means a sudden increase in starches, so most likely a dramatic increase in wheat-containing products;
A woman is more susceptible during the postpartum period because the immune system is trying to adjust to the body's changes following delivery;
A surgery, particularly in the gastrointestinal system, such as a gallbladder removal;
Certain viral infections; there is a possibility that antibiotics could serve as a trigger, but it is difficult to determine if the culprit is the infection itself or the antibiotic fighting the infection.

It is thought that stress and certain physical traumas could also be trigger factors. For many people, it is quite possible that no trigger is necessary; the symptoms just appear one day. Even more probable is the theory that the symptoms were there for a long time, but were simply ignored, masked or diagnosed as something else. People become accustomed to feeling tired or to having slight digestive disturbances. It is only when the problem worsens and becomes very distressing that they finally decide to seek medical help.

Symptoms of celiac disease

Celiac disease is difficult to diagnose as its symptoms vary enormously. Since symptoms are often subsequent of a lack of nutrient absorption in the small intestine, the list of problems can grow quite long. Gluten affects the permeability of the intestinal lining causing a leaky gut syndrome. This means that more intruders can sift through the intestinal lining, exposing the immune system to more allergenic substances than usual. This explains why celiacs tend to display more allergic symptoms that the population in general.

It is important to emphasize the fact that many victims of the disease are asymptomatic, even though the body's health is being consistently damaged. Often, the startling diagnosis of celiac disease is discovered quite by accident, following the investigation of another degenerative health concern or from a complication related to celiac which required a more in-depth examination. We will discuss the correlation between celiac disease and other health problems in chapter four.

Certain people exhibit classic symptoms such as diarrhea, digestive disorders, flatulence and bloating, but other signs are more difficult to relate to gluten intolerance, as is the case for anemia, irritability, vomiting and migraines.

Most common symptoms for infants and toddlers:
Diarrhea – often described by the parents as having a foul smell, a foamy appearance or stools that become abnormally abundant (4 or 5 times more than usual), soft, greyish in color and greasy in texture
Projectile vomiting
Distended abdomen
Lack of muscular mass or lack of muscular tone throughout the body
Failure to thrive
Dental disorders – ridges on the teeth or discoloured teeth enamel
Irritability, can become whinny and hostile
Listlessness, does not smile
Lack of appetite
Low blood levels of calcium, vitamin B12 and folic acid
Extreme separation anxiety or excessive dependence on the parents (probably because the child is in pain and is comforted by the parents presence).

Most common symptoms for children and adults:
Gastrointestinal distress – abdominal cramps, bloating, flatulence, discomfort, gastro-oesophageal reflux causing pain and burning (adult)
Diarrhea
Constipation
Steatorrhea (foul-smelling, frothy, sometimes floating stools)
Anemia or nutritional deficiencies
Ecchymosis (bruises)
Delayed onset of puberty
Lack of muscular mass
Weight loss
Lack of appetite
Chronic fatigue
Alopecia – temporary loss of body hair, partial or total
Emotional disturbances – irritability, depression, difficulty with concentration and excessive dependence.

In addition to these classic symptoms, others can be added to the list: very long eyelashes, premature hair loss, deformed fingers, amenorrhea (absence of menstruation), painful joints, tingling in the legs and feet, infertility, unjustified discomfort, mouth ulcers, and oedema (from a lack of protein). As research advances, the list of symptoms seems to lengthen, and now includes troubles with the liver, blood, articulations, teeth and even neurological dysfunctions.

The importance of a strict gluten-free diet has to be stressed. For the moment, a total exclusion of gluten is the only known solution to this disease, which will sap its victim's strength for as long as gluten remains in the diet.

Difficult to diagnose

A person going through a health assessment because of persistent symptoms will not easily be diagnosed with celiac disease and this for many reasons. Firstly, many people have only one or two symptoms. A doctor will prescribe the usual routine exams probably starting with blood work. If these results are normal, many patients will feel reassured about their health and will not demand further investigation. At a later time, when the same symptoms persist or amplify, they will return for a more in-depth examination. The patient's case may then be referred to a gastroenterologist (a doctor specializing in the digestive and intestinal systems). Once again, more tests will be performed, but not necessarily the right ones to uncover celiac disease.

Celiac disease comes about in different ways. It can be acute, subacute or insidious. A good example of its acute form is an infant showing classic symptoms such as diarrhea, vomiting and a distended stomach shortly after solids are introduced in his diet. In this case, the disease has a better chance for a prompt and accurate diagnosis.

In its subacute form, the condition can prove much more difficult to expose, as it strays from the classic description, with less obvious and less dramatic symptoms. For instance, a doctor examining a case history that describes the main problems as chronic constipation and anemia has no way to make the connection with celiac disease. We often tend to forget the difficulties a doctor can encounter in deciphering a condition. All too often, patients simply forget to mention certain symptoms such as chronic fatigue, restless sleep, joint pain or bowel irregularities, because they have become accustomed to living with them on a daily basis. An oversight of this kind further complicates a doctor's search. Frequently, a detailed case history can offer a better view of the whole situation.

The insidious form of celiac disease advances progressively and major symptoms only appear when the disease has already developed to the point of causing noticeable damage. It is often upon discovery of a different degenerative disease that further investigation sometimes leads to the detection of the celiac link. It is also very likely that the first condition will be treated without ever finding the underlying celiac disease. In that case, gluten will continue on his ravaging way and more related health complications will follow.

As you can see, the days when we merely trusted the medical system to put a label on our "aches and pains" are no more. Nowadays, with the unbelievable increase in autoimmune diseases (fibromyalgia, scleroderma, lupus...), we need to educate ourselves as to formulate more intelligent and precise demands upon the medical community. Medical testing will always be essential but it would be even more productive if the tests prescribed were those appropriate to our condition.

If we review the list of difficulties encountered in diagnosing celiac disease, we can see that all too often, the symptoms are imputed to other problems, that many doctors are still uninformed about celiac disease, and that the blood tests required to reveal the condition are not done systematically. Adding the necessary blood antibody testing to the routine workup would quickly guide the patient to the intestinal biopsy, if necessary, and to a definite diagnosis.

In the United States, pressure groups are asking the medical community to include screening for celiac disease in the routine blood work. This follows a series of trial-screening programs that took place throughout the country. It uncovered thousands of possible celiac sufferers who were directed towards more in-depth testing. Furthermore, the outcome of these screening programs is the reason why the real number of celiacs in the country is now being questioned. In Italy, where the disease is very common, children are routinely tested for celiac at age six. In Canada, blood testing is not done unless the disease is already suspected.

The following list was taken from the fall 1996 *Celiac Disease Foundation Newsletter*. It enumerates 20 conditions that are usually investigated by an allopathic doctor before exploring the possibility of celiac disease. It is obvious that many of these diseases have similar symptoms.

Anemia
Irritable bowel syndrome
Psychological stress, nerves, imagination
Diarrhea
Inflammatory bowel disease
Diabetes
Spastic colon
Ulcers
Virus (viral gastroenteritis)
Chronic fatigue syndrome
Weight loss
Allergies
Amoeba, parasites, infection
Gallbladder disease
Thyroid disease
Cancer, digestive lymphoma
Colitis
Cystic fibrosis
Lactose intolerance
Reflux.

Irritable bowel syndrome is one of the most commonly diagnosed intestinal disorders. It is estimated to affect between 8 and 20% of the population of Western countries. They alone make up for 25 to 50% of all referrals to gastroenterologists. It is reported in approximately twice as many women as men. Blood tests and other investigations usual show normal results. We could question whether some of these people actually suffer from celiac disease. Irritable bowel symptoms are very similar: abdominal pain, bloating, flatulence, diarrhea alternating with constipation, anxiety, phobia, weight loss and lactose intolerance.

Lactose intolerance is often related to gluten intolerance. It is hardly surprising that newly diagnosed celiacs also suffer from some degree of lactose intolerance, which is the inability to digest lactose, a sugar found in milk. Celiacs have a fragile small intestine due to the damaged villi precluding proper milk digestion. Lactase, the enzyme necessary to lactose digestion, is produced by the tips of the villi, so it is easy to conclude that if these are damaged by exposure to gluten, they are in turn incapable of producing a sufficient quantity of lactase. If the gluten-free diet is well abided to, dairy products can be returned to the diet after a few months on a trial basis. Once the small intestine begins to repair itself, the villi will heal and may be able to produce enough lactase to properly digest dairy products again.

It is important to mention that people can be lactose intolerant without suffering from celiac disease. It is a fairly common problem causing gas, bloating, abdominal cramps and diarrhea upon ingesting dairy products. It is estimated that it affects to some extend up to 70% of the world's adult population. Lactose is often an ingredient of other foods beside the obvious dairy source. Words to look for include whey, curds, milk by-products, dry milk solids, cream and non-fat dry milk powder.

If lactose intolerance becomes permanent, it is imperative to pay attention to calcium replacement. As dairy products supply calcium and vitamin D, we can use enriched soy, rice and almond milks as substitutes. Foods containing a lot of calcium are beans, green leafy vegetables such as broccoli and Chinese cabbage, black molasses, tofu, calcium-fortified orange juice, fish with edible bones (sardines, salmon), nuts and sunflower seeds.

Although it is not as common as lactose intolerance, it is also possible to suffer from sucrose and maltose intolerance. This will cause a carbohydrate malabsorption, and it is sometimes secondary to celiac disease though not often diagnosed. Carbohydrate intolerance is the inability of the body to completely process the nutrient carbohydrate (a classification that includes sugars and starches) into a source of energy for the body, usually because it lacks an enzyme needed for digestion. The enzyme necessary to digest sucrose (white sugar, brown sugar, syrups) is called sucrase. Maltase is the one needed to breakdown maltose (a by-product of starch). As seen with lactose intolerance, the damaged villi are incapable of producing proper enzymes for the digestion of carbohydrates. The symptoms are also very similar to those of lactose intolerance; they can include nausea and are mostly followed by diarrhea. They usually appear within thirty minutes to two hours after consuming carbohydrate-containing foods.

You can suspect sucrase and maltase deficiencies if after strictly adhering to the gluten-free diet for a period of time, you continue to suffer from cramps, nausea and diarrhea after eating carbohydrate foods such as gluten-free bread or sweets. If, on the other hand, you feel great after a protein-rich meal without carbohydrate ingredients, it may be interesting to repeat the experience and to observe if you obtain the same results. If so, avoid carbohydrates for a while to give the intestinal lining a chance to heal, and after a few months try a slow reintroduction of these foods. There is a good chance you will be able to tolerate them again.

The age factor

Celiac disease is not limited but an age barrier; it will strike people of all ages and of both sexes. Even though the symptoms can commence at any time after the introduction of gluten cereals in the diet, ages one to four are most generally targeted. In all decades of age, and even into the sixties, symptoms can manifest themselves at any time though they often come along after an event considered a trigger factor.

Upon the onset of puberty, symptoms of celiac disease sometimes seem to disappear. Specialists refer to this as "the honeymoon phase". Unfortunately, the condition never goes away, so this is a particularly dangerous phase for the teenager. The changes probably come about as a result of hormonal fluctuations, enabling certain celiac teens to tolerate small amounts of gluten without any or few outward consequences. This is a nightmarish period for concerned parents who are well aware that the intestinal damage is still happening with or without obvious symptoms.

A study involving celiac teenagers demonstrated that serological antibody screening did not reveal gliadin following gluten ingestion, even though a small bowel biopsy proved that there was significant damage to the intestinal lining. It concluded that testing for blood antibodies is not a valid marker during dietetic transgressions.[2] This honeymoon period can last for years; it can even continue well into the twenties. The importance of a stringent gluten-free diet must be emphasized to the teenager at the risk of repeating ourselves. Encouraging the teenager to consult with an empathic doctor may give more credibility to our parental concerns.

A study[4] published in 1995 suggested that celiac disease might be present in various forms. It established that the disease was more frequent in women, for whom the onset was often swift and violent. They stated: "The data also suggest the need to look for celiac disease in patients with unexplained hypochromic anemia. Except for asthenia, all signs and symptoms were more frequent in women than in men. Hypochromic anemia was the most common finding in women and was 40% more frequent in women than in men. Dyspepsia was twice as frequent in women as in men. Genital disorders were reported by 44% of women and by no men. Recent weight loss or low body mass index was the commonest finding in men. About 60% of men and women reported diarrhea; among patients without diarrhea, the prevalence of hypochromic anemia differed between sexes, occurring in about 80% of women."

The extent of the damage to the lining of the small intestine depends on the length of activity of the disease. As long as the disease stays unexposed, more villi will be flattened and rendered inefficient. From the moment gluten is completely withdrawn from the diet, significant healing of the intestinal villi is initiated. It may take from three to six months for younger celiac patients to heal, and as long as 2 to 3 years for older individuals. Improvement is often astonishing in children; not only do their symptoms disappear, but their behaviour can improve rapidly and they quickly catch up all growth retardation.

CHAPTER THREE

Digestion of gluten

To get a better understanding of the importance of proper gluten digestion and assimilation, we must recognize the irreplaceable role of protein in the survival of the human being. Gluten is a protein. Protein is composed of carbon, oxygen, hydrogen and nitrogen. It is the main component responsible for building and repairing body tissue. After water, protein is the most plentiful substance in our body. It constitutes about one fifth of our body weight. Protein is the main constituent of every living cell and of all body fluids except for bile and urine.

A continuous supply of protein is needed for cell building and regeneration. Good food sources of protein are meat, fish, eggs, dairy products, whole grains, beans and nuts. After ingestion, proteins are processed and broken down into amino acids.

There are 22 amino acids required to build protein, eight of which are considered essential. The essential amino acids must be provided through the diet as the body is incapable of manufacturing them. The remaining amino acids are classified as nonessentials and can be synthesized within the body. Amino acids are the final by-products of protein digestion. They are absorbed through the intestinal wall into the bloodstream and then circulate to our cells. This process is what keeps us alive. Our body cells can be very creative with amino acids. They use them to form structures in the shape of long chains, one link at the time. These chains are in fact new proteins endowed with specific capacities able to respond to all of the human body's needs. Each cell is made up of a mixture of proteins, and just one cell can contain hundreds of different protein patterns.

No one will ever presume to have perfect control over the human body, but each step towards better understanding of this complex machine points to the importance of doing our share to assure its preservation. One of the ways to ensure our body with quality care is to find the most favourable diet to our unique individual dietary needs. If we provide our body with its proper nutritional requirements, it will reward us by performing in a healthy and energetic manner. Let us now see where and how gluten digestion happens.

It all happens in the small intestine

A large part of gluten's digestive process takes place in the small intestine. Though called small, the description is not really accurate. If we could stretch it out to its full length, it would measure approximately 4.50 to 6 meters (15 to 20 feet). The duodenum is the first portion of the small intestine; it is connected to the inferior part of the stomach pouch. It measures about 20 to 25 centimetres (8 to 10 inches) in length and has a horseshoe shape encircling the head of the pancreas. It plays a fundamental role in digestion. It is the duodenum that receives the semi-digested food mass from the stomach through the pyloric sphincter. Bile is released from the liver and gallbladder if fats have been eaten, while the pancreas contributes alkaline pancreatic juices through the bile duct. These liquids are called biliary and pancreatic juices.

The duodenum connects to the jejunum, which is about 2.40 meters (8 feet) long. The jejunum is where useful foods are absorbed while leaving behind dietary waste and water. The ileum will then host the final stage of the digestive and absorption process. Each of these sections absorbs different nutrients through the intestinal wall. The duodenum absorbs calcium, vitamin A, thiamine and riboflavin, while the jejunum absorbs fats, and the ileum absorbs vitamin B12.

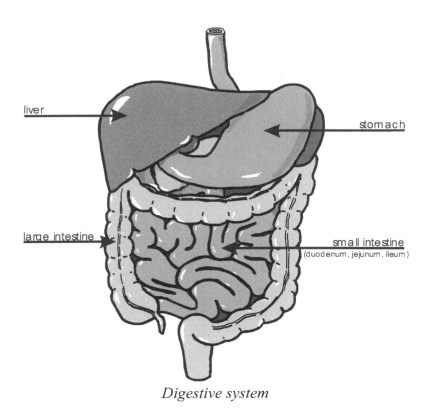

liver

stomach

large intestine

small intestine
(duodenum, jejunum, ileum)

Digestive system

The ileum is the most tortuous part of the small intestine, measuring approximately 2.4 meters (8 feet) long. It is attached to the large intestine or colon by a circular valve called the ileo-caecal valve.

The role of the small intestine is paradoxical as it serves a double function. It must let nutrients pass into the bloodstream while blocking the absorption of large molecules such as non-digested gliadin, microbes and toxins. Its barrier consists of only one layer comparable in thickness to that of an eyelash. Alcoholic beverages, food allergens, medication and stress can cause irritation and inflammation to the intestinal mucous membrane. This can lead to many problems. Once this barrier is compromised, the intestinal lining loses its ability to filter intruders; it simply leaks, as well

37

described by the term "leaky gut". Symptoms of all kinds can appear when this filter allows the entrance of irritants.

When one suffers from gluten intolerance, it is the small intestine that is affected. Damage starts in the duodenum following the arrival of a gluten-loaded food mass, and then spreads to the jejunum. If the condition persists, the ileum will also be impaired. In the active phase of celiac disease, absorption of all nutrients will be diminished. The spread of the damage to the intestine and the period of time between the beginning of the disease and the time of diagnosis will determine which nutrients will be less well absorbed. As a rule, the more severe the damage is, the more absorption is altered and deficient.

What happens during digestion?

The gastrointestinal tract is quite a complicated affair; now that we have an idea where the digestion of nutritional elements takes place, let us see how it happens. Digestion represents a series of physical and chemical changes, by which each food ingested in the body is broken down and reduced to mush, subsequently prepared for intestinal absorption, to then be oriented towards the circulatory system.

Digestive juices start to flow even before the first morsel of food enters the mouth; the smell and sight of a meal plate suffice to awake the whole process. Digestion begins in the mouth while chewing reduces the big pieces of food to swallowable size. Immediately, ptyalin, an amylase enzyme in saliva, coats the food and begins to breakdown starches into simple sugars. Upon swallowing, the food continues its voyage down a long tube called the oesophagus, into the stomach where digestion will go on for at least another hour. In the stomach, gastric juices, containing enzymes (pepsin, rennin), water and hydrochloric acid, assist protein digestion, as well as that of fats and other substances. The strong layers of muscles in the stomach will churn the food into a paste called "chime".

The chyme will enter the small intestine in the following order: sugars, followed by proteins and then fats, which are slower to digest. Nutrient absorption takes place in the small intestine after a continuous digestive process that requires up to three hours. Absorption is the method by which nutritive elements in their simplest forms are chosen and assimilated by the intestine to be directed towards the bloodstream to insure cellular metabolism. To be accessible at a cellular level, nutrients will have to be broken down as follows: proteins into amino acids, carbohydrates into simple sugars (glucose), and fats into fatty acids.

It is at this point of the digestive process that the individual with celiac disease begins having serious problems.

What are villi?

The small intestine is in fact the one that nourishes each one of our cells by permitting the passage of nutrients through the bloodstream. If replenishment of nutrients is not consistent, cells cannot function properly. Consequently, what goes on in those minute little cells directly affects how the individual feels. A deficiency in nutritional elements will eventually result in physical and psychological symptoms.

Essential nutritional elements — proteins, vitamins, minerals and fats —, are absorbed through hundreds of ridges or leaf-like folds, termed intestinal villi, which normally cover the intestinal mucosa. Many digestive enzymes are present on the surface of the villi in the jejunum. These enzymes usually complete the digestive process of carbohydrates and proteins.

Each villus measures about one millimetre and is visible to the naked eye. The area over which digestion and absorption take place is increased by the villi, for each small hair-like projection has millions of small microvilli resembling fingers. It could also be compared to a thick bath towel where each thread can be seen separately. With more than five million microvilli, the surface available for absorption could cover 9.30 square metres or 100 square feet.

Continuous exposure to gluten-containing foods in a person with celiac disease destroys the villi. Similar to hair or to the bristle of a hairbrush, the villi are responsible for the absorption of nutritive elements. Eventually, under the influence of gluten, the villi become partially or completely flattened and incapable of doing their job. The term "villi atrophy" is often used to describe this intestinal damage. While this goes on, the body is deprived of essential nutrients, and symptoms appear sooner or later. The damage to the villi is completely reversible by eliminating all gluten-containing foods.

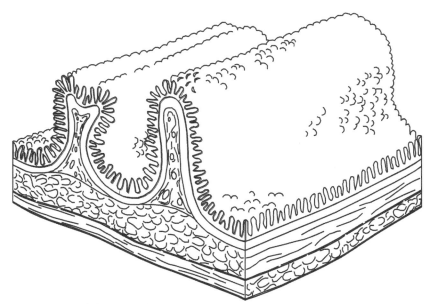

A section of the small intestine showing the intestinal villi

Diagnosing the disease

Victims of celiac disease can be divided in two separate groups. There are the ones showing classic symptoms of the disease and whom a gastroenterologist generally diagnoses within a reasonable period of time. The second group exhibit atypical symptoms, which make the condition very difficult to pinpoint. It is not a matter-of-fact job to detect celiac disease in a person complaining mostly of depression and headache while showing no digestive symptoms. These symptoms do not even require a consultation with a bowel specialist.

The elaboration of a complete case history by a comprehensive doctor is of vital importance. The questionnaire should also include health facts concerning all immediate family members. The consultation will most likely lead to a series of blood tests resulting in further medical investigation, and if you are in luck, to a quick and accurate diagnosis. The idea of a gluten-free diet for the rest of one's life or for our child can be terrifying at first, but this diagnosis is still easier to accept than many others. Once the newly diagnosed person or parent realizes that the condition requires no difficult treatment, medication or surgery, relief is great, and learning to deal with a gluten-free diet and possibly a few months of vitamin supplementation seem a small price to pay to reclaim ones health.

Blood screening

Although looking for specific antibodies in the bloodstream to detect celiac disease is not always conclusive, it is a good screening method. Only the small intestine biopsy can ascertain or refute the diagnosis of celiac disease. Current diagnostic methods include blood testing to detect blood antibodies although the results can be misleading. Specifically, the doctor will be searching for the following antibodies: anti-gliadin (AGA) of the type IgA and IgG, anti-reticulin (ARA), anti-endomysium (EMA), and anti-tranglutaminase (tTG).

Depending on where you live, the serological tests prescribed by the doctor will vary among these. In the United States, blood screening for celiac disease is used more often than in Canada, but it is also possible that its use in Canada is simply less publicized.

In the United Stated, the anti-gliadin antibodies blood testing is the most commonly used. The laboratory will search for two types of

41

antibodies: the antigliadin IgA and IgG. They readily react to gliadin by fighting it as though it was an enemy in the body. Antireticulin antibodies can also be evaluated though it is a less sensitive test than the others so considered less trustable. The degree of damage to the intestinal lining usually correlates to the level of antireticulin antibodies in the blood.

An endomysial antibody testing (EMA) is specific to celiac disease. The immune system of people with celiac disease reacts by making these antibodies when gluten is ingested. The endomysial antibodies attack the endomysium, which is an intestinal tissue. That means that if the person does not have celiac disease, the test result should be negative; if it comes back positive, the likelihood of having the disease is very high. The small bowel biopsy will follow to confirm the diagnosis.

Testing for anti-transglutaminase antibodies (tTG) is relatively recent. It is known that gluten contains a lot of glutamine, an amino acid, which is particularly vulnerable to a reaction with transglutaminase. The physiological function of transglutaminase, which is an enzyme, is probably to repair tissues damaged by inflammation. Therefore, if the intestine is damaged in the presence of gluten, there will be a reaction between glutamine and the transglutaminase enzyme. According to Dr. Joseph Murray of the Mayo Clinic, this test may soon replace the gliadin and endomysial testing.

A very important factor to remember is that to have an antibody response, the person has to continue on a gluten-containing diet. Once gluten is withdrawn from the diet, antibody levels drop quickly and testing would be inconclusive if not worthless. All of these tests are not uniformly available; it always depends on the medical system of each province, state or country. In the United States, privately owned laboratories even promote some of these services on the Internet. Whether or not blood screening results point to celiac disease, if you strongly suspect that you suffer from gluten intolerance, find a doctor willing to do the intestinal biopsy.

Small bowel biopsy

A small intestine biopsy is the most adequate and accurate way to diagnose celiac disease. The test must be performed while the patient is still consuming wheat and other gluten-containing grains in his diet. If gluten has been excluded from the diet for even a short period of time, the biopsy will be useless as the intestinal lining can heal fairly quickly.

The objective of a jejunal biopsy is to discover and evaluate the degree of villi atrophy or damage. The biopsy can be carried out under general anesthesia or awake (light sedation will be offered), depending on the patient's age and preference. The test used to do the biopsy is called an endoscopy. A small flexible tube named endoscope is inserted into the mouth, through the oesophagus and stomach, and threaded to the small intestine. The end of the tube has a small metallic capsule pierced with a tiny hole. Small specimens of the intestinal mucous membrane are aspirated through the orifice; this procedure is painless as there are no pain-sensitive nerves inside the small intestine. The specimens are sent to the laboratory for analysis. A positive diagnosis of celiac disease is substantiated if the results demonstrate atrophy or flattening of the villi. Treatment in the form of a gluten-free diet can then begin.

It is important to be aware that a small bowel biopsy can implicate a few risks as all invasive procedures can. Recognizing these will allow a clear-minded decision. Although it is a simple intervention, if the patient has chosen to be anesthetised, there is always a small chance of complications. Another incidence of difficulty, though rare, is the risk of perforation of the small intestine. There could also be a problem with excessive bleeding.

As a biopsy draws only a small specimen of the intestine, the possibility of obtaining a healthy sample from a celiac bowel is not altogether impossible, especially is the disease has not yet damaged a very large surface. Besides, a skilled and conscientious doctor is needed to carry out this delicate analysis, as the damage may be difficult to detect if it is minimal. The foremost goal is to avoid a false negative, which would condemn an uninformed celiac patient to continuous suffering.

Unfortunately, a small bowel biopsy can reveal healthy intestinal tissues even with a history of gluten intolerance and an increased permeability of the intestine (leaky gut), caused from constant irritation and inflammation. If this is the case, we are back to the starting point with annoying symptoms, even incapacitating for certain people, and with no diagnosis in sight.

Going gluten-free

We did a quick review of a gluten-free diet in chapter two, and we will elaborate on the subject in chapter five. For people with a confirmed diagnosis of celiac disease, the dread of a serious illness such as cancer and the fears propagated by a fertile imagination will subside with time, and peace of mind will return. The removal of all glutenous foods from the diet often brings about quick and spectacular results. For certain individuals, the road to recovery will be a bit longer, depending on the degree of damage to the intestinal villi and the strictness of adherence to their gluten-free diet, but undoubtedly, with patience and willpower, victory is within reach.

Many cities all over the world now offer support groups and associations for celiacs, and with the growing accessibility of computers and the Internet, hundreds of websites filled with information and recipes are within everyone's reach.

Unfortunately, many individuals receive a negative biopsy result while they strongly suspect that they suffer from gluten intolerance.

When the situation is doubtful, one can decide to avoid all gluten-containing foods on a trial basis. The idea is to eliminate all dietary gluten for a period of six to twelve weeks, though most specialists agree that two to six months is a more realistic time-frame before expecting to see signs of improvement. If there is a remission of disturbing symptoms while on a gluten-free diet, it is most likely that these individuals really suffer from gluten intolerance.

All too often, following a negative test result, the individual returns home and continues to eat the same offensive foods. A doctor who relies solely on the biopsy result is dogmatic and less scientific, as after all, a patient's welfare should be of the uppermost importance. A broad-minded doctor would suggest a gluten-free diet for a trial period and subsequent assessments. However, we must add that many patients prefer to believe the test results, as undertaking a special diet represents a considerable effort for an already weakened person.

The challenge test

The "challenge test" is sometimes recommended to people with an uncertain diagnosis. After eliminating gluten-containing foods for a few months, it is added back to the diet. Intolerance symptoms can reappear as quickly as in a day or two, but they can also take a few months to return so it is important to be attentive to how one feels. The short period of time without symptoms is explained by the fact that the intestinal lining has started to heal. Symptoms return when damage to the villi is reactivated. If this is the case, a lifetime exclusion of gluten in the diet is the only advisable solution.

Many physicians agree that the best way to ascertain a celiac diagnosis is to do a series of intestinal endoscopies to biopsy the small intestine. After the initial biopsy, a second one is suggested after a few months without gluten, and then a third one after the gluten challenge test has been done. This approach is becoming less popular as a small intestine biopsy does implicate a few health risks.

Many people simply refused to undertake the challenge test at this time as they are finally starting to feel healthier.

The challenge diet is not recommended for celiac teenagers during their "honeymoon period", a time when symptoms seem to go into remission. If you are doubtful of your biopsy results, there is no danger in initiating a gluten-free diet, even without your doctor's approval. Gluten-free foods are not detrimental to good health; it is rather a different and sometimes quite imaginative way of eating. Let us remember that celiac disease does not yet have a cure, only a diet solution.

The main danger in trying the challenge test is that for one reason or another, some people do not return to the gluten-free diet, even after the recurrence of celiac symptoms. Whether the reason is mere laziness, a lack of confidence in the diagnosis, a reluctance to follow a specific diet, or because this person has atypical symptoms difficult to relate to an intestinal disease, it does not matter; we must offer this person moral support and information without being judgmental.

In reality, the diagnosis of celiac disease must include these three factors:

A suspicion of celiac disease based on symptoms, physical appearance, delayed growth (in children) and abnormal blood tests;

A small intestinal biopsy, which shows damage to the villi and the presence of immune system markers typical of celiac disease;

A definite improvement with a gluten-free diet.

If gluten consumption persists

A wrong diagnosis of the condition or a celiac patient refusing to adhere to the gluten-free diet can be dangerous, even life-threatening.

Without a complete avoidance of glutenous foods, the celiac person will gradually progress to one or many disabling degenerative conditions. These celiac sufferers will eventually become undernourished, deficient of many essential nutritional elements, anemic, lethargic, and definitely uncomfortable, especially if they suffer from intestinal symptoms. Infertility has also been attributed to this disease.

According to Dr. Joseph Murray[1] of the Mayo Clinic, since celiac disease is an autoimmune disease, it follows that other diseases of the immune system can be associated with it. Rheumatoid arthritis, lupus, type 1 diabetes and some eye problems are a few examples of conditions more frequently seen in celiac patients. He adds that these diseases are not caused by gluten ingestion or by celiac disease itself, but rather by a genetic predisposition to immune system problems. Celiacs have 60 to 80 times greater chance of suffering from an intestinal lymphoma, a type of cancer extremely rare in the general population.

The risk of developing lymphoma immediately begins to decrease when a celiac victim eliminates gluten from the diet. The risk continues to decrease for a period of three to five years, until is approaches that of the general population. Dr. Murray believes that people with celiac disease should avoid gluten as if it were rat poison!

Symptoms of malabsorption

Exposure to the gluten-containing protein in a person with celiac disease destroys the villi of the intestinal mucosa; the term "flat" is often used to describe them at this point. Without villi, the inner surface of the small intestine becomes less like the thick towel mentioned above and more like a naked tile floor. The loss of villi causes in turn a loss of digestive enzymes, as well as a reduction in surface area for absorption. As a result, foods of all types (not only gluten-containing foods) tend to pass through the intestinal tract without being completely digested.

Usually, passage of partially or undigested foods through the intestinal tract causes diarrhea. There is often undigested fat in the stools of people with celiac disease; bowel movements tend to be bulky, of grayish colour, and have an extremely foul smell. They sometimes float in the toilet with visible droplets of fat around them; undigested foods can also be seen.

If the loss of non-digested food into the stools continues over an extended period of time, weight loss could follow as both body fat and muscle mass will diminish. Clinical signs could include a bloated stomach, thin arms and legs and flat buttocks. Celiac children seem less inclined to abdominal cramps, instead they have a tendency to become irritable and lethargic. Although their physical appearance is that of starved children, they actually have little appetite for food.

Celiac disease will quickly converge to malnutrition if a treatment to cease the malabsorption process is not promptly established. Vital nutrients that should feed our body cells through the bloodstream are lost in the stools; eventually there is a genuine shortage of nutritional essentials. As fat is lost through the stools, it brings about a loss of calcium. A lack of calcium can in turn lead to kidney stones or to a bone disease called osteomalacia, which is a softening of the bones in the adult, the equivalent of rickets in children. Malnutrition can cause noticeable growth delay in children and seriously hinder development.

A shortage or malabsorption of certain nutritional essentials can lead to many consequences in the body:

Carbohydrates:
If they are not digested properly or if absorption is impaired, these sugars stagnate in the intestinal tract, are broken down by the intestinal flora and end up as acid residue, which is harmful to the human body.

Proteins:
Proteins undergo a process similar to carbohydrates, but perhaps worse. Nutritional loss is increased yet again as the intestinal wall can exude protein rich secretions.

Fats:
Fat is lost in the stools. Little if any is absorbed as it should. For a healthy person, there is about 5 grams of fat excreted in the stools for a 24-hour period. For the celiac individual, this number can easily go up to 20 grams. This factor is also considered when making a celiac disease diagnosis.

Calcium:
As mentioned above, hypocalcemia can result in neurological and bone problems.

Vitamin K:
A lack of this vitamin can lead to problems with blood coagulation.

Iron, B complex vitamins including folic acid:
They are all vital to red blood cell synthesis. A deficiency can lead to blood complications such as anemia.

And the list could go on to include all vitamins as well as many essential minerals. In addition to solving the absorption problem by starting a gluten-free diet, it is important to revitalize the individual by adding a supplement of vitamins and minerals for a few months, until the intestine has return to par and can resume its vital functions. The epithelial cells of the intestinal villi are capable of quick renewal, which is of great importance. The epithelium is known to renew itself every three to six days. This means that with a gluten-free diet considered as a priority, intestinal health can be restored rapidly.

CHAPTER FOUR

Conditions connected to celiac disease

Celiac disease is an autoimmune disease. "Autoimmune disease" is a general term referring to a state in which the human body produces immune reactions against itself. A better understanding of how the immune system works will help us grasp that concept.

The immune system is composed of specialized cells, which identify and eliminate intruders that threaten human health. To be more specific, these intruders are bacteria, viruses, parasites, fungi, and cells that have become abnormal (cancer) or used up. Hungry immune system cells quickly label them as undesirable and devour them. If this were not the case, these intruders would multiply at will and our health would soon deteriorate.

Sometimes, the reaction of the immune system is too aggressive. This is what causes an allergic reaction. An allergy is an inappropriate and excessive response from the immune system to a normally inoffensive substance (pollen, dust) to the human body.

When a person suffers from an autoimmune disease, the immune system attacks itself, targeting its own cells, tissues and even its organs, as if they were foreign intruders. Examples of autoimmune diseases include lupus, sarcoidosis, multiple sclerosis, psoriasis, diabetes and arthritis.

White blood cells, also called lymphocytes, are the backbone of the immune system. We can divide white blood cells into several categories, but the two most important ones are the B-cells, which secrete antibodies to fight off foreign invaders, and the T-cells, which participate in the immune reaction by mounting an efficient attack against any enemy trying to infect body cells with a virus, or cancer cells. T-cells also rid us of cold viruses and other threats from outside the body.

The T-cells from the intestine of people with celiac disease respond specifically to something in gluten, identifying it as a substance that must be eliminated from the body. To be more explicit, the T-cells react to the part of gluten that is linked to a human body protein called transglutaminase. As a result, lymphocytes, which usually prevent any damage in the body, do the exact opposite when tranglutaminase is present; they attack the intestinal villi.

The immune systems of celiacs, as well as those of all victims of autoimmune diseases, are hyperactive, and not as it is often believed, in a state of diminished activity. If these people are often ill, it is due to malnutrition caused by malabsorption of essential nutrients rather than to a poor immune system.

Complications caused by gluten intolerance

In the previous chapters, we enumerated the numerous symptoms of celiac disease, and discussed the short-term consequences of a lack of absorption of essentials nutrients. We will now explore the numerous complications brought on by a prolonged malabsorption problem due to gluten intolerance.

Without a definite withdrawal of all gluten-containing foods, celiac disease will continue its ravages and can cause many important and even life-threatening conditions which include:

Osteoporosis − a condition where the bones become weak, brittle and predisposed to fractures. Poor calcium absorption is a contributing factor to this condition;

Osteomalacia − a softening of the bones in the adult caused by a lack of absorption of vitamin D. An osteomalacic component is found in

50 to 70% of celiac victims[1]. A diagnosis of celiac disease is often made following an investigation of a previous diagnosis of osteomalacia. The equivalent in children is rickets;

A short stature in children from a lack of essential nutrients from a young age, a time when proper nutrition is crucial to growth and development. When the condition is detected and treated before the end of puberty, growth retardation may be caught up;

Bone pain or arthritic pain;

Weight loss;

Epilepsy with cerebral calcifications or convulsions – can result from an inadequate absorption of folic acid. It is thought that a lack of folic acid causes calcium deposits called calcifications to form in the brain, which in turn cause seizures;

Internal hemorrhaging;

Central and peripheral nervous system disorders;

Pancreatic problems;

Lymphoma and adenocarcinoma (types of intestinal cancer);

Anemia;

Chronic diarrhea;

Lactose intolerance;

Recurrent oral aphthous ulcers;

Lack of dental enamel formation in children;

Infertility in both men and women;

In women, delayed onset of menstruation, premature menopause, miscarriage and congenital malformation of the baby at birth such as neural tube defect;

A variety of emotional problems such as chronic fatigue, irritability, inability to concentrate, attention deficit disorder with or without hyperactivity, and even schizophrenic behavior.

Other people at risk who should be tested

Once a diagnosis of celiac disease is confirmed, all members of the immediate family should be tested even if they do not exhibit any symptoms. As it is a genetic disorder, one or both of the parents are at least a carrier of the gene. A carrier is a person that passes a particular gene on to his children but doesn't have the disease. Many studies estimate that more than 10% and some presume up to 30%, the chances that immediate family members, also called first-degree relatives, may have celiac disease with or without symptoms. It is important to remember that the disease may stay dormant in certain individuals until a trigger factor intervenes. Do not be surprised if asymptomatic relatives bluntly refuse the investigation. After all, who wants to be told they are sick. The thing to do is to explain the consequences the disease could have on their long-term health if it stays undiagnosed. They will then have the necessary knowledge to make a clear-minded decision.

People suffering from certain health problems should be tested whether or not they have family members diagnosed with celiac disease and even though they do not exhibit any symptoms. Certain autoimmune diseases seem to have a preference for celiacs. These conditions do not cause celiac disease; the increased probability of developing one of the diseases listed below is most likely related to the same hereditary factors that predispose to celiac disease. Following a gluten-free diet will not stop the onset of these diseases.

People diagnosed with the following conditions or all other autoimmune disease should be tested:

Type 1 diabetes mellitus (insulin dependant)

Irritable bowel syndrome

Inflammatory bowel disease

Persistent iron deficiency

Down syndrome

Cystic fibrosis

Chronic hepatitis or liver cirrhosis

Acquired Immune Deficiency Syndrome (AIDS)

Thyroiditis

Scleroderma

Nephropathy (renal problem)

Sjogren syndrome

Raynaud syndrome (circulatory problem)

Addison's disease (adrenal insufficiency)

Myasthenia gravis

Rheumatoid arthritis

Epilepsy.

Conditions possibly associated to celiac disease

Since celiac disease is still considered as rare in North America, its symptoms are often wrongly diagnosed as irritable bowel syndrome or lactose intolerance. According to Dr. Joseph Mercola[2], the true incidence of celiac disease is much higher than we think. He estimates that one out of ten people could suffer from it. He firmly believes that wheat is one of the primary reasons why people get sick in this country. He is astonished by how many chronic health complaints clear up once wheat is removed from the diet. Some researchers speculate that few people can properly digest the wheat protein. Our body attempts to breakdown this protein by attaching an enzyme to it. For a high percentage of people, the enzyme-gliadin complex stimulates an autoimmune reaction that can cause celiac disease or more frequently, a variety of chronic health complaints, most of which are intestinal.

Though there are still more questions than answers about gluten intolerance, links between gluten consumption and several diseases and conditions are being brought to light.

Autism

Autism belongs to a larger group of disorders identified as pervasive developmental disorders. It is a condition, more pronounced in some than in others, resulting in a behavorial disorder that begins in childhood and that lasts a lifetime. These children tend to isolate themselves from others, often preferring to live in a world of their own, showing little interest for the outside environment. This behavior is emphasized by other traits such as an avoidance of eye contact, a lack or slow speech development and an inability to socialize or to form emotional bonds with others. Many people with autism engage in repetitive activities like rocking or banging their heads. Some have a predilection for ritual gestures such as drinking from a specific cup and therefore show resistance to change. Autonomy and learning are also affected.

For a long time, autism was associated with psychiatric disorders. Nowadays, a new approach is being considered as specialists are investigating a connection between autism and the immune and gastrointestinal systems. Recent research advocates the importance of nutrition in the treatment of autism. Various studies have established a link between the general aggravation of autistic behavior and certain food intolerances. Among the main culprits are casein, a milk protein, and gluten.

Around 1980, several papers debated the correlation between diet and autism. Since then, many studies confirmed that 50% of autistic patients see their condition improve while on a gluten-free and casein-free diet. In the newspaper *Le Soleil* of May 13th 2001, an article by nutritionist Josiane Cyr, even mentioned a percentage of betterment of 81%. She added that Dr. Bradstreet, an American doctor, claims that a gluten and casein-free diet should be the first step to consider with autistic children, as the results are better if started at an early age.

Casein has a molecular structure that is nearly identical to that of gluten. This could possibly explain why the absorption of both proteins causes similar problems. It was suggested that if the digestive system were incapable of metabolizing certain proteins such as casein and gluten, it would retain a certain amount of partially digested peptides (amino acids). A more recent theory supported by many studies contends that these peptides could have opioid properties (of the same chemical family as morphine). This opioid effect could disorganise numerous central nervous system functions such as perception, emotions, behavior and humour. Researchers have concluded that many peptides from incomplete food breakdown could pass through a permeable intestinal lining (leaky gut), and make their way to the brain through the bloodstream, where it would provoke considerable damage resulting in known autistic symptoms. It was also noticed that autistic children have a marked attraction for foods containing these two proteins, comparable in fact to people addicted to opioid drugs.

These observations led to more research in the United States, Great Britain and Norway. All registered an abnormal occurrence of opioid peptides in the urine of a large percentage of autistic individuals. Evidence of elevated levels of an opioid-like substance was also found in the cerebro-spinal fluid of some children with autism, especially in those who exhibited different behavorial characteristics; they either appeared to feel less pain than the normal population, or they had a tendency towards self-injurious behavior. Again researchers concluded that these opioid-like substances could only be derived from the incomplete breakdown of certain foods.

Let us now backtrack to the reason why peptides are able to cross the intestinal lining in the first place. According to Josiane Cyr's above-mentioned article, which was published after the international convention on autism in Quebec, autistic subjects frequently suffer from chronic intestinal inflammation. She describes a study from 1996 which included 21 individuals suffering from autism; as many as 43% of them showed an increased permeability of the intestine. Upon further examination, all 12 children showed intestinal abnormalities.

For people who want to submit to in-depth diagnostic testing for celiac disease, it is important to remember to do these tests before withdrawal of gluten-containing foods, or else the results will be negative.

It cannot be ascertain that a diet modification towards a gluten-free and casein-free one will cure autism, but if there is a chance of improving behavorial response in a percentage of autistic children, consequently bettering life quality of both child and parents, it may be worth the effort. Some autistic children, diagnosed before the age of two and adhering to this diet ever since, have responded so well to the change that their diagnosis is now questionable. In children who try the casein and gluten-free diet when they are older, results may not be as obvious, but each step towards progress is important. Improvement in adults has also been documented.

Once the dairy-free and gluten-free diet is underway, there may be withdrawal reactions such as an upset stomach, anxiety, anger, temper tantrums and a tendency to be more dependent. These symptoms should be considered as a good and positive sign. Over a period of three months, some or hopefully many signs and symptoms of autism may diminish or disappear. If there is no change after a period of three months, there most likely won't be any. Thousands of parents throughout the world have confirmed positive changes in their children and in some cases, remarkable improvement. Some high functioning autistic adults describe it as having the fog lifted.

Depression

Many studies report depression as a very common symptom of celiac disease. Anyone who was once afflicted by depression for even a short period of time can imagine how awful it would be to sustain it long-term without being able to determine its cause. Depression is characterized by a persistent feeling of sadness and lethargy, which abates all desire and courage necessary to face daily activities, and sometimes affects even the will to live. There are many causes to depression such as the loss of a loved one, a hormonal imbalance, an allergy or a nutritional deficiency.

In a book entitled *Coeliac disease* (1984), Cooke and Holmes repeatedly cite depressive illness as the most common symptom of gluten intolerance. They add that the newly diagnosed celiacs recover from their depressive state much more quickly if their diets are supplemented with vitamin B6. They go on to explain that when the jejunal villi are damaged by celiac disease, it does not only disrupt fat soluble vitamins absorption but also that of vitamins B6, B12 and folic acid, which are all implicated in neurotransmission.

In another trial, eleven celiacs suffered from persistent depression despite being on a gluten-free diet for more than two years.

However, after supplementation with vitamin B6 at 80 mg per day for six months, all signs of depression disappeared.[3]

In 1999, yet another study demonstrated that untreated celiac disease could lead to serious behavorial disorders. A pediatrician described three adult patients with undiagnosed or untreated celiac disease, showing no intestinal signs but exhibiting persistent depressive symptoms. These adults were the parents of pediatric patients. For all three, symptoms of depression lifted when gluten-containing foods were withdrawn. He concluded that celiac disease should be considered in the presence of behavorial and depressive disorders, particularly if they are not responsive to the usual antidepressive therapy.[4]

Another report observed a variation in urinary peptides in psychotic depression. It described the same kind of peptides excreted in the urine of depressed individuals, but in greater quantity than normal.[5] We know that psychotic depression often includes hallucinations, which is also the case with opioid consumption. We can question whether opioid properties affect the brain as it is suggested with autism. If the quantity of urinary peptides is greater, could the hypothesis that a greater amount of opioid-like substances is released in the brain be plausible?

Whatever the explanation, any type of depression is difficult to deal with. For people still in search of an answer to a persistent depressive state, the idea of investigating celiac disease is a trail of hope (see Emily's testimonial in chapter nine). A trial-period of three to six months on a gluten-free diet is strongly encouraged with or without conclusive celiac testing.

Dermatitis herpetiformis

Dermatitis herpetiformis, also referred to as Duhring's disease or Duhring-Brocq, is a chronic and benign skin disorder associated with celiac disease. There is strong evidence that the changes in the intestinal mucosa and immunologic findings in the majority of patients are identical to those described in celiac disease. Also, gluten seems to be correlated to the skin rash, which occurs with dermatitis herpetiformis. This would explain why dermatitis herpetiformis is often referred to as "celiac disease of the skin" while celiac disease is called "celiac of the gut".

Typically, the disease starts in the teens or in the third or fourth decade of life. It is estimated to affect one in 100 000 people with a ratio of two men for one woman. It is more common in white people and rather rare in the Black and Asian population.

Characteristically, dermatitis herpetiformis starts with a severe burning sensation and a prickling of the skin that causes intense itching different from an ordinary itch. These unpleasant sensations can be perceived eight to twelve hours before the actual lesion appears. The new lesion is red, elevated, usually measures less than a centimetre in diameter, and contains a vesicle or a blister in its center that is pus-free. If the lesion is scratched, a scab will form on its surface. The itch can persist for seven to ten days before vesicles start to scab. Body areas that are usually targeted are the elbows, the knees, the neck, the shoulders, the upper back and the buttocks. The face is occasionally affected but the inside of the mouth rarely is. It is common for the lesions to be symmetrically distributed on the body.

The word herpetiformis is derived from "like herpes", because these lesions tend to appear in groups like the herpes lesions. As there are many skin conditions with similarities, a biopsy of the skin lesion is necessary to attain an accurate diagnosis. It is still unknown why all celiacs do not develop the skin disease. The damage to the jejunal villi is essentially the same in the two diseases, except that it is usually more severe in celiacs. It is important to note that only a small percentage of dermatitis sufferers actually show gastrointestinal symptoms, although from 14 to 20% suffer from fat or iron malabsorption or a combination of the two. They also have a higher incidence of pernicious anemia, thyroid related diseases and intestinal lymphoma.

The treatment plan includes medication for the dermatitis, though it will have no effect on the damage to the intestinal villi. A gluten-free diet must be established immediately. It is also suggested to avoid all dairy products since they seem to exacerbate the disease. Dermatitis herpetiformis is considered a lifelong disease, although severity may wax and wane. Remission may occur in 10 to 20% of patients.

Diabetes

Insulin dependent diabetes, also called juvenile or type I diabetes is an autoimmune disease in which the body's white blood cells attack and destroy the cells from the pancreas that are responsible for manufacturing insulin. Since a diabetic body cannot produce enough insulin, it must be injected regularly. Of all autoimmune disorders associated with celiac disease, the best-known connection is the one between celiac and type I diabetes.

According to a study done in Oxford by Dr. John Todd, type I diabetes affects about one percent of the general population, but five to ten percent of celiacs. Diabetes is usually diagnosed before celiac disease, mostly because diabetes symptoms show up early in a child's life and its diagnosis is very evident. The two diseases show some similarities, such as a preference for descendants of European origin and identical immune system markers. To date, no connection has been established between celiac and type II diabetes (adult onset type).[6]

Another study brought to the public's attention in October 2001 corroborates that approximately five percent of diabetic children also suffer from celiac disease. Dr. Steven L. Werlin and his colleagues, from the Medical College of Wisconsin in Milwaukee, tested 218 diabetic juveniles aged between four and twenty-one, and a control group of 117 children of the same age for anti-endomysium antibodies. Patients with positive results were offered a small bowel biopsy. Their symptoms were also assessed by a questionnaire given to the parents. Seventeen of the diabetic children tested positive for endomysial antibodies, but none among the control group. Fourteen of these seventeen patients underwent a small bowel biopsy. Villous atrophy was found in eleven of them. Two patients had increased intraepithelial lymphocytes without villous atrophy. Interestingly, more than half of the diabetic children diagnosed with celiac disease were asymptomatic. According to Dr. Werlin, these results indicate that there is a connection between celiac disease and juvenile diabetes. Another study presumes that treating celiac disease would render diabetes easier to manage. It recommends that all children suffering from diabetes be tested for possible celiac disease, as this could prevent many of its complications.[7]

Down syndrome

Down syndrome is caused by a chromosomal abnormality; for some unexplained reason, an accident in cell development results in 47 instead of the usual 46 chromosomes. This extra chromosome changes the orderly development of the body and brain. It is usually responsible for mental retardation and other abnormalities. Prominent facial features including a flattened nose, a protruding tongue, and upward slanting eyes characterize Down syndrome. Congenital heart defects are frequent as well as gastrointestinal abnormalities and immune system deficiencies.

Recent studies indicate that Down syndrome children are more at risk of developing celiac disease that the general population. Though the reason for this is not entirely clear, it is thought that these children are at greater risk for autoimmune diseases in general, and celiac disease is simply one of them. Studies from Europe show that the percentage of children suffering from both Down syndrome and celiac disease ranges from seven to sixteen percent.

Dr. Susan L. Neuhausen and her associates, at the University of Utah School of Medicine in Salt Lake City, studied 97 trisomic children, aged from two to eighteen years old. Ten of these children tested positive for celiac disease. According to the results of genetic testing on these children, their genetic predisposition was the same as that of the general population, which led the researchers to believe that a gene on chromosome 21 might be involved in the pathogenesis of celiac disease. The only symptom exhibited by this group of children was bloating. It was concluded that children with Down syndrome should be screened for celiac disease because there is a 10% incidence of this autoimmune disorder in the trisomic population.[8]

Migraine headaches

A migraine is a severe and often recurrent headache, which can greatly perturb one's life. Dr. Marios Hadjivassiliou, a British neurologist, has studied this subject for many years. In a study published in the February 2001 journal of Neurology, he states that gluten can trigger migraines in gluten-sensitive people who do not exclude it from their diets. For this study, he examined ten adult patients who had a long history of persistent headaches that were resistant to treatment. Some of these patients also suffered from additional symptoms such as a lack of movement coordination and walk perturbation. A blood screening was done to find antibodies specific to gluten; all of these patients tested positive, therefore indicating that they suffered from a hypersensitivity to gluten. They also underwent magnetic resonance imaging (MRI), which showed inflammation of the central nervous system. Nine of the ten individuals went on a gluten-free diet, and seven of them stopped having migraines completely. The other two patients also obtained partial relief. One of these patients was forty-five years old and suffered from headaches since childhood. According to Dr. Hadjivassiliou, eliminating gluten from the diet may be a promising therapeutic intervention for people with chronic headaches.

Multiple sclerosis

Multiple sclerosis is a debilitating neurological disease, which affects coordination, vision and language. It can appear and progress rapidly. This progressive perturbation of the nervous system affects people between the ages of twenty and forty and exceptionally after age fifty. Women seem to fall victim to multiple sclerosis more often than men. The destruction of the nerve's myelin sheaths in the brain and spinal cord causes the symptoms of multiple sclerosis. What brings about this disease is still unknown though many possibilities are being mentioned such as hereditary factors, a viral or bacterial infection, an autoimmune component and even nutritional factors.

Several studies suggest that nutrition is a very important factor. Many individuals afflicted with multiple sclerosis seem to improve when they reduce saturated fats and supplement with essential fatty acids. There is probably more than one dietary factor implicated. Researchers have demonstrated that symptoms diminish when allergenic foods are identified and eliminated from the diet.

Dr. R. Shatin of Alford Hospital, in Melbourne, Australia, has suggested that an inherited susceptibility to multiple sclerosis is from a primary lesion in the small intestine caused by gluten intolerance, and that demyelination of the nerve sheaths is, in fact, secondary. He also implied that the high incidence of the disease in Canada, Scotland and western Ireland might be associated to the predominant consumption of Canadian hard wheat, which has the highest gluten content of all wheat varieties. He adds that Africans who prefer millet, a non-gluten grain, have a very low incidence of multiple sclerosis.[9]

A large number of people firmly believe that their symptoms diminish and are kept under control when on a gluten-free and milk-free diet. Roger MacDougall was diagnosed with multiple sclerosis in 1953, in London, by one of the world's leading neurologist at the time. Within a few years, MacDougall was unable to use his legs, fingers or his eyes. Even his voice was affected and he was unable to stand up for more than a few seconds. He recovered his health by eliminating gluten, milk products, animal fat and sugar from his diet. His eyesight was restored and he returned to leading a normal life including running up and down stairs. Twenty years after he was diagnosed, a neurologist from the United States gave him a thorough neurological examination and confirmed that he suffered from multiple sclerosis. Nevertheless, MacDougall fully enjoyed the rest of his life and was still asymptomatic when he died as an octogenarian.

Once again, the importance of diet and of early detection of food intolerance is emphasized. Gluten intolerance can be difficult to detect especially in celiacs with atypical symptoms; it is often by educating oneself and by questioning doctors, nurses and dieticians that an answer can be uncovered.

Osteoporosis

Osteoporosis results from a progressive bone loss, which diminishes the bone's density and thickness. In an advanced state, as the bones become more brittle, osteoporosis can lead to fractures, most often of the vertebras, hips and wrists. Since bone mass is built mostly from childhood to the mid-twenties, it becomes crucial to detect celiac disease as early as possible.

People who are gluten intolerant also suffer from osteoporosis because of a calcium deficiency. Again, we must remember that vitamin and mineral absorption takes place in the small bowel; this is also where the villi are under attack in celiac disease, therefore reducing the absorption of all nutrients. If gluten is not withdrawn from the diet, calcium will not be the only nutrient to be poorly absorbed; we will also have a problem absorbing fat-soluble vitamins, including vitamin D, which plays an essential role in calcium assimilation and utilization.

Calcium absorption is critical in the formation of children's bones. A lack of calcium and vitamin D can slow or stunt bone development, leading to physical growth retardation. The good news is that once gluten is excluded from the diet, and as the small intestine heals and absorption reactivates itself, a child can start catching up on lost time. Children's growth will pick up rapidly and depending on the child's age at the time of diagnosis, all growth retardation can often be caught up. Bone tests have demonstrated that bone density can return to normal in children. Some doctors will recommend calcium supplements for a period of time.

Osteoporosis in the adult is considered mostly irreversible. Bone density loss is accelerated during menopause and post-menopause. Once again, detecting celiac disease as quickly as possible is imperative. As soon as the condition is controlled by a gluten-free diet, it is time to fulfil nutritional deficiencies. Amongst other vitamins and minerals, a calcium formula is essential; it must also contain magnesium, phosphorus and vitamin D to ensure proper absorption. A good rule of thumb is a 2:1 calcium to magnesium ratio. Physical activity such as walking and weight lifting are greatly encouraged to help maintain bone health. According to Dr. John Lee, in his book *What your doctor may not tell you about menopause*, natural progesterone cream may have a positive effect on osteoporosis. He states that it may increase bone density in women of all ages.

Osteoporosis is often referred to as the silent disease since very few symptoms are associated with it. Loss of bone density and the brittleness of the bones that ensue do not produce symptoms in themselves. The discovery of osteoporosis is often secondary to a broken bone. When one is diagnosed with celiac disease, it is important to verify bone health. This is done very simply with a test called bone densitometry or osteodensitometry, which detects osteoporosis. It is painless and easily accessible with a doctor prescription. The bone densitometry should be done when celiac disease is first uncovered and again in a year or two to better evaluate changes in bone density.

Rheumatoid arthritis

Rheumatoid arthritis is a chronic inflammatory disease that often has an insidious outset. Initial symptoms usually appear between the ages of twenty and forty, though it can set in at any age including childhood. Statistics indicate that it is three times more common in women than men and it affects about one to three percent of the population. Rheumatoid arthritis may manifest itself slowly. It is characterized by fatigue, early morning joint stiffness, as well as pain and inflammation in symmetrically located joints. The inflammation attacks the synovial membranes of the joints and can wander from joint to joint throughout the whole body. The disease can advance to the stage of invalidating ankylosis.

Rheumatoid arthritis is definitely an autoimmune disease and although the trigger factor is still unknown, there are many hypotheses. A virus, a genetic susceptibility, a dietary factor or an increased permeability of the intestines have been mentioned.

Dr. R Shatin of Melbourne, Australia, has explored the possibility that gluten may be a factor in rheumatoid arthritis. He suggested that the primary lesion of the disease is in the small intestine, where malabsorption caused by gluten intolerance predisposes the individual to the condition.[10]

Many studies have demonstrated that intolerance to wheat as well as to other foods can trigger important disturbances in the human body.

For example, wheat has been linked to distressing inflammatory symptoms. Signs of wheat allergy include painful joints, particularly in the hands, accompanied by slight swelling and stiffness.

The mechanisms set in motion by the ingestion of wheat in rheumatoid arthritis victims have been studied. They seem to follow several steps to finally reach the joints and cause inflammation. A researcher by the name of Little[11] and his colleagues believe that it all begins with a permeable gastrointestinal tract that lets through certain protein antigens (a substance identified as foreign to the human body that provokes the production of antibodies by the immune system) derived from gluten digestion, in this case, gliadin. This antigen appears in the bloodstream and is bound to a specific antibody (protein substance produced by the body in reaction to the presence of an antigen). This antigen-antibody complex then activates the rest of the immune response and serotonin is released from the blood platelets. Once serotonin flows through the bloodstream, it causes symptoms as it circulates to joint tissues. The joints are then more or less under attack by the antigen-antibody complex, which causes damage to joint cells and activates inflammation. More inflammation results in more pain, oedema, stiffness and a loss of mobility. While this chain reaction due to gluten antigens has been verified by many studies, it is known that other food allergens can also trigger arthritis.

A study published in the British medical journal, *The Lancet*[12], in 1989, evaluated the long-term evolution of 112 individuals diagnosed with rheumatoid arthritis and treated by conventional medicine. After twenty years, only 18% of these people still had a normal lifestyle, 35% were deceased and 19% were severely handicapped. For most cases, death was directly related to rheumatoid arthritis. These results clearly demonstrated that conventional treatments are not effective in long-term management of the disease. It is urgent that we find other methods of healing.

Many sufferers of different forms of arthritis are aware that diet is implicated as much in the cause of their disease as it is in the treatment. People with arthritis should demand to have their blood screened for celiac disease, and even proceed to the intestinal biopsy before they remove glutenous foods from their food list. In the event of a negative diagnosis, the diet should be reviewed to include more high fiber foods, while diminishing meat and sugar intake. Eliminating all gluten-foods for a period of three months or more is well worth a try. If the avoidance of these foods could offer some kind of relief, it would seem to be a simple, inexpensive and very encouraging avenue to explore.

Schizophrenia

Schizophrenia affects approximately one percent of the population and exists worldwide. The condition develops slowly over many months, usually beginning in adolescence or young adulthood. The individual becomes disconnected from reality; his thought pattern is disturbed, his affectivity is disrupted, perception and behavior are altered. This person can sometimes feel persecuted. A distorted perception of life brings on changes in personality, tension, depression, fatigue and hallucinations, which in turn result in isolation.

Research over the years has cited many causes to schizophrenia: heredity, complication at birth, head trauma, secondary reaction to a virus and heavy metal poisoning. Dr. Carl C. Pfeiffer, a pioneer in the field of nutritional research, wrote in his book *Nutrition and Mental Illness*, a list of twenty-nine causes to the condition, from the well-known to the practically unheard of. Some of the causes mentioned were hypothyroidism, vitamin B12 and folic acid deficiency, heavy metal toxicity, hypoglycemia, cerebral allergy, wheat-gluten sensitivity, chronic infection from *Candida Albicans* and serotonin imbalance.

Undiagnosed celiac disease can simulate symptoms alike those of schizophrenia. It is known that gluten intolerance can modify a person's state of mind even as far as to bring on a severe depression. Schizophrenic behavior in certain individuals has been known to improve after a period of fasting; it was then questioned whether a food allergy could be the culprit. Unfortunately, the effect of food and the link between body and mind are still much neglected in the traditional therapeutic approach, so the connection between food allergy and mood disorders often goes unnoticed. According to Dr. Pfeiffer, evidence is accumulating that links various psychiatric disturbances with grain malabsorption.

Dr. Lauretta Bender reported one of the earliest observations on the subject in 1953. She noted that schizophrenic children were extraordinarily prone to celiac disease. By 1966, she had reported twenty such cases among two thousand schizophrenic children. [13]

These observations were brought to the attention of Dr. F. Curtis Dohan[14] of the Medical College of Pennsylvania. He was studying the numerous biochemical associations of schizophrenia. As early as 1966, he noted that schizophrenia occurred more often than by mere chance in children and adults with celiac disease. He observed common behavioral disturbances in both children and adult celiacs on a gluten-containing diet. These agitations subsided after the introduction of a gluten-free diet. He added that often, during periods of psychic stress or acute infection, the severity of celiac disease symptoms increased. In some cases, the schizophrenic symptoms seem to augment as well.

Dr. Dohan suggested that in gluten intolerant people, gluten might enter the brain and affect the nerve receptor sites. He suspected that peptides from gliadin were the substances that traveled from the intestine to the brain. After a few more years of research, he stated: "Similarly, considerable evidence indicates that the major cause of schizophrenia is the inborn inability to process certain digestion products of some food proteins, especially cereal grain gluten..."[15]

Dr. Dohan recommends complete abstinence from gluten-containing grains as well as from dairy products since they seem to have a similar effect. This trial period should last from six months to a year. It is possible to wait weeks, perhaps even months to witness marked improvement. When gluten–containing grains and milk products are reintroduced, there is usually a relapse towards schizophrenic behavior whether in months, weeks, or sometimes even hours. It is then imperative to maintain a strict adherence to the gluten and casein-free diet.

Another case of interest was found in Italy. A thirty-three years old patient, with a pre-existing diagnosis of schizophrenic disorder, consulted for severe diarrhea and weight loss. Anti-endomysial antibodies were present in blood serum and a jejunal biopsy showed villous atrophy. A gluten-free diet was started, resulting in the disappearance of psychiatric symptoms and normalization of intestinal findings. This was the first case in which an undiagnosed and untreated celiac patient with psychiatric manifestations had his symptoms disappeared after a gluten-free diet. More so, this could be verified by a before and after brain tomography that proved the disappearance of a dysfunction of the frontal cortex.[16]

It appears that in individuals with a certain genetic predisposition, gluten is capable of producing schizoid alterations in the personality. Though it should not be insinuated that gluten causes schizophrenia, would the hope of a return to normalcy in a schizophrenic person not be incentive enough to try a gluten-free diet?

Spontaneous abortion and fetal growth retardation

There are two potential risk factors for women who carry an unsuspected case of celiac disease and who want to get pregnant. The first one is a higher chance of infertility when compared to the average woman, and the second is a higher risk of having a baby with an important birth defect. Further research shows that men may also have infertility problems as a result of celiac disease.

For women who have celiac disease without knowing it, the most likely explanation for increased birth defects is that they lose a lot of nutrients through malabsorption, a problem they don't even suspect. These women assume that since they are eating an adequate diet, they are fulfilling all of their nutritional requirements. In fact, they could be lacking essential nutrients such as folic acid and iron, which play a critical role in fetal development. Folic acid is indispensable, especially at the beginning of the pregnancy, while the expecting mother may not even know she is pregnant. A deficiency in folic acid is one of the main factors in the development of neural tube defects such as anencephaly (absence of a brain) and spina bifida.

Many studies have demonstrated that proper diagnosis of celiac disease and complete withdrawal of gluten can greatly affect the final outcome of pregnancy. In Italy, in March 2000, a research concluded that up to 50% of untreated celiac women suffered miscarriages or an unfavourable outcome of pregnancy. In most cases, after six to twelve months on a gluten-free diet, this percentage was brought back to normal. [17]

In 1996, another study that took place in Naples, Italy, investigated the effect of a gluten-free diet on the outcome of pregnancy and lactation in 125 celiac women. This research came to the conclusion that a gluten-free diet in women with celiac disease can positively affect pregnancy, consequently diminishing the incidence of spontaneous abortion, of low birth weight babies, and of short breast-feeding periods. [18]

According to a recent study done in 2000, by Dr. Antonio Gasbarrini and his colleagues in Rome, celiac disease may play a role in recurrent spontaneous abortion and intrauterine fetal growth retardation. The researchers studied 44 patients with a history of spontaneous abortion, 39 patients whose fetuses showed intrauterine growth retardation, and 50 women with no problems (control group). For each group, blood testing was done to evaluate serum concentrations of anti-endomysial and anti-transglutaminase antibodies (indicators of celiac disease). According to Dr. Gasbarrini, the patients with recurrent spontaneous abortion and those with intrauterine fetal growth retardation had a significantly higher frequency of serological markers than controls. Further, they found that three patients with recurrent miscarriages and six of those with babies showing intrauterine growth retardation tested positive for celiac disease. These nine women underwent the jujenal biopsy and eight were positive for celiac disease. Amongst these eight patients, three showed chronic inflammation of the duodenal mucosa and a nearly total villous atrophy, while five others presented severe mucosal (intestinal lining) atrophy. They concluded once again of the importance of proper recognition of celiac disease as a risk factor for miscarriage and intrauterine fetal growth retardation.[19]

Men who have an infertility problem associated with celiac disease can often reverse the difficulty by adhering to a gluten-free diet, giving them a chance to experience paternal bliss after all. Studies demonstrate that infertile women following the same dietary approach might also be able to conceive.

It is important to mention that celiac women maintaining a gluten-free diet during pregnancy do not encounter additional risks related to the disease. Of course, prenatal medical visits as well as vitamin and mineral supplementation are always recommended as for all pregnant women.

As research about autoimmune diseases moves along, we realise that there is a long way to go before we understand the extraordinary complexity of the human body. One thing is for certain; nutrition has a place of choice in the prevention and healing of diseases. A correlation is now being considered between food allergies and health conditions such as fibromyalgia and chronic fatigue. Since people afflicted with these conditions often suffer symptoms similar to those of celiac disease, should we interrogate ourselves on a potential connection between them? Only further research and discoveries will shed light on the matter.

CHAPTER FIVE

The diet

It goes without saying that one cannot live without food. Nevertheless, in our modern world, nutrition is about to become an important obstacle to optimal health. While animals possess a natural instinct to choose the most suitable food for survival, the human species, possibly blinded by so-called modernization, has lost that innate intuition. When men were compelled to choose their food depending on seasonal availability, there was a healthy and natural rotation of foods. Nowadays, with all sorts of foodstuff easily accessible, more and more degenerative diseases are making their appearance forcing us to review our ostentatious lifestyle.

The addition of pesticides to our crops and a large assortment of additives to our foods are not without worrisome consequences on our state of health. No one can predict what long-term effects these products may have on the human body, and it should not be excluded that daily absorption of such poisons could cause a potentially harmful accumulation in the body.

Could there be a definite connection between the drastic increase in food intolerances and allergies, and what our plate really contains? Food consumed at a meal can provoke the death of thousands of immune cells in the hours following ingestion, resulting in a marked lack of vitality and vigilance on the part of the immune system. Although this is a simplified look at an intricate matter, it is easy to imagine the consequences that could ensue, such as a degeneration of the immune system, and the remarkable arrival of more and more complicated conditions, particularly, autoimmune diseases.

A gluten-free diet is the only recognized solution to celiac disease. Though it seems to be fairly simple at first glance, it often becomes a living-nightmare for many people. Fortunately, support groups are multiplying; they provide dietary information, and most importantly, moral support to the celiac population. Let us now have a closer look at the permitted and forbidden foods, as we try to unmask this famous protein.

Grains to avoid

The problematic grains for the gluten intolerant are enumerated in chapter 2. When we first look at the list, is seems quite easy to eliminate a few cereals from our diet, but when we examine each ingredient more closely, it gives the impression that we live in a world made exclusively of gluten. Very often, newly diagnosed celiacs feel panicky at the simple thought of grocery shopping, a situation made even worse if their child is the person they have to shop for. No well-intentioned parent would want to poison their child, nonetheless, this is exactly how gluten reacts in a celiac prone body. Much trial and error, research and reading will be necessary to demystify this glutinous world.

Firstly, gluten-containing grains are wheat, rye, oats and barley. As nothing could be so straightforward, we have to add their derivatives, which are triticale, a hybrid of rye and wheat, and wheat's close relatives, spelt and kamut. Spelt and kamut are delicious and nutritious varieties of wheat, but they contain the noxious gluten protein, which means they are stamped with a forbidden seal to all celiacs.

Certain individuals add spelt to their diets. They are often celiacs with less severe intestinal symptoms or those who may have less damage to the intestinal villi therefore permitting some assimilation. Since this grain is easily digestible, they may suffer no immediate symptoms. People who have followed a gluten-free diet for a while and are now asymptomatic may also repeat this scenario. It is important to remember that despite the fact that symptoms are nonexistent for a time, damage to the inner lining of the intestine and to the immune system is still happening for as long as gluten is present. Studies have determined, with unquestionable evidence, that spelt and kamut contain gluten and are harmful to the well-being of gluten intolerant individuals. Though it can be comforting to think that one has outwitted the disease for a time, long-term repercussions on one's health are just too high a price to pay.

A gluten-free diet excludes all foods that contain the grains enumerated above as well as their derivatives:
Cereals made of these grains;
Foods and beverages made of these grains;
Foods cooked with these grains;
Processed foods containing gluten under any of its many appellations;
All foods containing gluten in a form that may be more difficult to expose.

The following list is only a partial list of foods to be careful of:
Most products from a bakery, even if prepared with gluten-free flour, as there is a risk of cross-contamination from gluten-containing foods (breads, pancakes, brioches, croissants, pretzels...);
Pastries (cakes, pies, donuts...);
Pastas (spaghetti, macaroni, lasagna...);
Most breakfast cereals (All bran, oatmeal...);
Most infant cereals;
Most crackers (soda cracker, Ritz, Bretons...);
Beer, coffee from cereals, Postum, etc.;
Seitan (vegetarian food);
Meats, fish, onions or all foods that are coated with flour or bread crumbs;
Meatloaf or fish loaf which often contains bread crumbs;
Gravies, sauces, soups and desserts thicken with wheat flour (béchamel sauce, cream of mushroom soup...);
Delicatessen products, liver pâté, sausage, etc.;
Sauces of all sorts including soya and tamari sauce;
Many canned preserves and dry soup packages;
Many herbal mixes, spices or seasonings, certain brands of pepper, icing sugar, instant coffee, margarine;
Certain brands of ice cream and yogurt;

Communion host.

To avoid gluten completely, one must become a detective and also learn a different language, as ingredient labels often seem to be written in a foreign dialect. Many words or expressions designate gluten. We must also be cautious of labels indicating the mention "wheat-free". It is important to know that "wheat-free" does not signify "gluten-free". If the product was made in a glutinous environment without special precautions, it could be contaminated or one of its ingredients could be a derivative of wheat. It is possible that an ingredient mentioned in the list below is not made from one of the offensive grains; many have been included because food formulas change constantly.

This general list of ingredients containing gluten (to be avoided) is extracted in part from "Forbidden List", courtesy of www.celiac.com:

Anti-caking agent
Baking soda *****
Barley
Beer
Bran
Brown flour
Brown rice syrup (often from barley)
Bulgur wheat/nuts
Calcium caseinate*
Caramel color (can contain wheat)
Cereal binding
Citric acid
Couscous
Dextrins***
Durum wheat triticum
Farina Graham
Filler
Gravy cubes
Ground spices

Gum base
Hydrolyzed plant protein (HPP)
Hydrolyzed vegetable protein (HVP)
Icing sugar
Kamut
Malt
Malt extract (barley)
Malt flavoring
Malt syrup
Malt vinegar
Meat flavoring
Miso *****
Modified food starch
Mono and diglycerides ****
Monosodium glutamate (MSG)*****
Mustard powder
Oats
Oat bran
Rye
Semolina
Soba noodles*****
Sodium caseinate*
Soya sauce*****
Spelt
Starch******
Stock cubes*****
Tabbouleh
Triticale
Wheat germ
Wheat starch**

*   May contain monosodium glutamate (MSG).
**   Most celiac organizations in Canada and United States do
not believe that wheat starch is safe for celiacs. In Europe, however,
where wheat starch is of higher quality than generally available in

Canada and the United States, it is considered acceptable by most doctors and celiac organizations.

***   Dextrin is an incompletely hydrolyzed starch. It is prepared from dry heating corn, waxy maize, waxy milo, potato, arrowroot, WHEAT, rice, tapioca or sago starches.

****   Mono and diglycerides can contain a wheat carrier in the USA. While they are derivatives of fats, carbohydrates chains may be used as a binding substance in their preparation, which are usually corn or wheat, so this needs to be checked out with the manufacturer.

*****   Can utilize gluten containing grain or by-product in the manufacturing process, or as an ingredient.

******   For products manufactured in the United States, the word "starch" always means, "corn starch". It is not always so for other countries.

Wheat represents about 80% of our grain consumption. Currently, it is estimated that food manufacturers use 74 kilograms (163 pounds) of wheat per person each year. This represents a considerable increase comparatively with 62 kilograms (137 pounds) per person in 1972. Grains are indirectly invading human food through animal feed. Livestock and poultry now have grains added to their food rations. This practice started when grain was cheap, and it persisted when owners realized that this diet encouraged quicker animal growth, allowing animals to reach markets quickly and profitably. It has been questioned whether or not grains added to animal feed could possibly cause a health risk to the gluten intolerant individual consuming these meats. This proves once again the pressing need to inform and educate people around us about the dilemma that people with celiac disease face each day.

Oats controversy

Oats toxicity for people suffering from celiac disease was established in the 1950's, at the same time as that of wheat, barley and rye. It was only

82

in 1995 that this hypothesis was challenged. It would seem that oats is closer genetically to corn and rice, which are permitted to celiacs, than to wheat. There is also a debate as to whether or not oats is contaminated by crop rotations, where the same fields are used alternatively for oats and wheat, and by the utilization of the same harvesting material and stocking facilities. Though minimal, the risk of contamination does seem to exist.

Most celiac associations still exclude oats from the gluten-free diet. Although the subject was discussed in chapter two, it seems pertinent to return to it briefly. Many studies have demonstrated that adding oats to a gluten-free diet is appropriate. A recent research done over a period of five years by Dr. Matti Uusitupa and his colleagues, from the University of Kuopio in Finland, studied the long–term effects of adding a moderate amount of oats in an otherwise gluten-free diet for adult celiacs. In a previous study, no harmful effects were detected after celiac patients ate oats for twelve months, which was reflected by the patient's symptoms, nutritional status and duodenal villous condition. It also showed that ingestion of oats did not delay recovery of mucosal damage in newly diagnosed celiacs.

Dr. Uusitupa continued his study and went on to compare the results of a gluten-free diet and a gluten-free diet that included oats. He selected 92 adults with celiac disease, which he divided in two groups: 45 individuals whose intake of oats averaged approximately 34 grams a day in an otherwise gluten-free diet, and 47 patients in the control group whose diet was gluten and oats free. After five years, 35 patients in the original oats group, 23 of whom were still eating oats at least twice a week, and 28 in the control group that was on a conventional gluten-free diet were examined. The results confirmed that eating oats did not cause any duodenal mucosal damage to the adult celiac patients. Furthermore, blood screening showed no negative effects that could be linked to eating oats

According to Dr. Uusitupa, the high antibody levels that appeared in some of the patients that were in both groups are most likely explained by poor compliance to a gluten-free diet. He believes that the reason why oats can be tolerated by celiacs must be based on structural differences between the proteins in oats, wheat, barley and rye. The toxic portion of gluten is gliadin, whose toxicity remains even after digestion. It is possible that the specific amino acid sequence that is found in wheat gliadin is not found in oats avenin, which would explain why oats can be assimilate by celiacs. The researchers also add that taking oats off the list of forbidden foods might improve patient compliance to the gluten-free diet by giving them more food choices.[1]

More and more studies are available on the oats debate. In summary, though the hypothesis of oats toxicity was invalidate since 1995 by numerous researches, most celiacs still avoid it, dissuaded of its safety by so many ambivalent theories.

Sprouted grains

Although sprouting grain increases its digestibility and nutritive value, sprouted wheat still contains gluten. Sprouting activates the enzymatic process that begins to breakdown wheat's gluten into amino acids. This process is not sufficient to eliminate all gluten contained in the sprouted grains. Therefore, even in a sprouted form, all gluten-containing grains must be excluded from the diet. However, non-gluten sprouted grains are of great benefit to good health. Add sprouted buckwheat to a salad; its rich color and flavor will tickle your taste buds, while its numerous nutrients will boost your immune system. Many grains and seeds can be used for sprouting including sunflower, lentils, fenugreek and radish. Do not let this easy way of revitalizing your body pass you by.

Reading labels

Now that we are acquainted with the forbidden foods and ingredients in a gluten-free diet, let us have a look at the permitted additives. As additives are often appointed very peculiar names, it is reassuring to be able to distinguish which ones are gluten-free. It is very important to realize that certain additives entail considerable health risks. The following list should in no way be considered a blessing to use more additives; it is simply meant to shed light on gluten-free dietary choices. The final decision about protecting our health by proper nutritional choices belongs to each individual. It is impossible to issue a complete list of gluten-free additives as they are too numerous, and their formulas change all the time with no previous notice. Also, new ones are added regularly. The following list is an extract of "Safe List – Foods and Ingredients Safe for a Gluten-Free Diet", a courtesy of www.celiac.com:

Acacia gum
Adipic acid
Agar
Algin
Alginate
Allicin
Aluminium
Annatto color
Arabic gum
Ascorbic acid
Aspartame*
Aspic
BHA (butylated hydroxyanisole)
BHT (butylated hydroxytoluene)
Benzoic acid
Beta carotene
Biotin
Butyl compounds
Calcium carbonate
Calcium chloride
Calcium phosphate
Calcium silicate
Calcium stearate
Camphor
Caprylic acid
Carboxymethylcellulose
Carnauba wax
Carob bean gum

Carob flour
Carrageenan
Casein
Castor oil
Cetyl Alcohol
Chlorella
Chymosin
Citric acid**
Collagen
Corn sweetener
Corn syrup solids
Cortisone
Cotton seed oil
Cysteine, L
Dextrimaltose
Dextrose
Dioctyl sodium
Elastin
Ester gum
Folic acid or folacin
Formaldehyde
Fructose
Fumaric acid
Gelatin
Glutamic acid
Glutamine (amino acid)
Glycerides
Glycerol monooleate
Glycol
Glycolic acid
Guar gum
Hemp
Hydrogen peroxyde
Hydrolyzed soy protein
Iodine
Invert sugar

Keratin
Lactic acid
Lactose
Lanolin
Lecithin
Lipase
Magnesium carbonate
Malic acid
Microcrystallin cellulose
Magnesium hydroxide
Maltitol
Mineral oil
Mineral salts
Monopotassium phosphate
Monosodium glutamate (USA)
Musk
Niacin – niacinamide
Oleyl Alcohol/Oil
Paraffin
Pepsin
Peru balsam
Phenylalanine
Polyethylene glycol
Polyglycerol
Polysorbates
Potassium citrate
Potassium iodide
Propolis
Propyl gallate
Propylene glycol monosterate
Pyridoxine hydrochloride
Rennet
Reticulin
Royal jelly
Sodium acid pyrophosphate
Sodium ascorbate

Sodium benzoate
Sodium citrate
Sodium erythrobate
Sodium hexametaphosphate
Sodium lauryl sulfate
Sodium nitrate
Sodium silacoaluminate
Sodium stannate
Sorbic acid
Sorbitol - mannitol*
Soy lecithin
Sphingolipids
Stearamide
Stearamine
Stearates
Stearic acid
Sucrose
Sulfites
Sulfosuccinate
Sulfur dioxide
Tallow
Tartaric acid
TBHQ ou Tributylhydroquinone
Thiamine hydrochloride /vitamin B1
Tolu balsam
Tragacanth
Tragacanth gum
Tri-Calcium phosphate
Tyrosine
Vanillan
Vitamin A (palmitate)
Whey
Xanthan gum

*   Can cause irritable bowel symptoms

**   All citric acid produced in the United States is made from corn. Other sources of citric acid may be made from sugar cane, dextrose, corn or WHEAT.

Permitted grains

Now that your knowledge of glutinous grains is up to date, the time has come to continue our stroll towards a more positive topic. Let us turn our attention to permitted grains. When wheat is removed from the diet, it seems as if there are no acceptable grains, cereals or flours left in our kitchen cupboards. However, with a bit of patience and imagination, a world of new flavors and textures is awaiting. It is difficult for us to conceive that elsewhere in the world, wheat is not perceived as the only available grain.

The following grains and starches are permitted to the celiac population. Even if these substitutes do not contain gluten, some people can still react negatively to their ingestion, just as it is possible with any other food. It is preferable to add only one new food staple to the diet at the time and to evaluate its effect. If in doubt, simply remove the suspected offensive food from the diet for a few months, and repeat the experience later.

Rice
Corn
Soya
Potato
Buckwheat
Quinoa
Millet
Amaranth
Teff
Arrowroot
Sorghum
Manioc (tapioca)
Job's tears
Ragi

Sago
Nut flour

With our fast paced lifestyle, experimenting with new recipes catches the interest of only a small percentage of the population, and gaining knowledge of new grains with unusual names and learning how to cook them bothers the daily routine. Nevertheless, it is known that appetite comes while eating. As we become familiar with these "ancient" starches, our taste buds must adapt to new flavors, very different than that of wheat. Of course, to become acquainted with each new grain or starch can demand a bit of initiative, patience and tenacity, but as for all new experience worth its while, the discovery of various succulent dishes will gave you great satisfaction.

Amaranth comes from a Greek word meaning "immortal". The Aztec culture was sustained for centuries by amaranth. It was in 1521 that Cortez, a Spanish conqueror, dominated the Aztec Empire of Mexico and banished amaranth as a commercial crop. It almost vanished from the face of the earth. Although it was no longer cultivated, the hardy seeds survived four and a half centuries in the wilds of South and Central America and Mexico. In 1972, a team of botanical researchers found wild amaranth growing in Mexico. They collected some seeds and experimented growing them at the Rodale Research Center in Eastern Pennsylvania. It was a great success. Amaranth was back in the picture.

Amaranth contains more iron than most plants. Historians speculate that this is the reason why the Aztec Indians survived a drought year without succumbing to starvation. The amaranth grain contains enough nutrients to preserve life except for vitamin C. As the Aztecs also ate the amaranth leaves, they obtained the necessary vitamin C as well as other nutrients, and were able to resist famine. Amaranth has more protein than other grains (16 to 20%); it is rich in lysine, an essential amino acid of which most grains are deficient. Its protein is more complete than the one in milk or soya bean. It is also an excellent source of fiber while containing calcium and other minerals. Its nutritive proprieties make it a food of choice for vegetarians and celiacs.

Preparation: For a hot cereal with a nutty taste, cook 250 ml (1 cup) of amaranth seeds in 2 1/2 to 3 times more water; simmer at low heat for 15 to 20 minutes. For a texture closer to that of rice, add two times more water than grain. It can also be used as flour in some recipes. It is advisable to keep it in the refrigerator to avoid rancidity.

Corn is a cereal originating from America, probably from Mexico or Central America. It was a main food staple in pre-Columbian civilizations on most of the continent. The myths of Mayas, Aztecs and Incas often referred to corn; it had its place in their religious ceremonies, served as trading currency, and its silks were used as tobacco. From Mexico to North America, cornmeal sweetened with honey or served with vegetables, meat or fish was a well-recognized dish. Corn is still very popular. It is sometimes called "maize" or "Indian corn", probably because this continent was thought to be the Indies when it was first discovered.

Cooked corn is an excellent source of folic acid, potassium and thiamin. It also contains magnesium, pantothenic acid, vitamin A and C, phosphorus, niacin, zinc and riboflavin, while providing loads of fiber. However, it is deficient in lysine and tryptophan, two important amino acids. Corn is available under many forms such as yellow corn semolina with whole grains, corn flour, corn bran and cream of corn. It also makes excellent pasta. Corn is often transformed and added to food as cornstarch, corn syrup, dextrose, fructose and glucose.

While corn is accepted in a gluten-free diet, it is still a very allergenic food for many people. Furthermore, it can be irritating to those with a more delicate digestive system. For celiac sufferers with severe intestinal symptoms, it is preferable to wait until the intestine has regained some kind of normalcy before introducing corn to the menu. By respecting a short waiting period, you will avoid the false impression of being intolerant to yet another food, while in reality the body just needs to recuperate before handling such a grainy food. Corn flour is less irritating to the digestive system than corn on the cob, which is very fibrous. When it is well tolerated, corn is an interesting choice for celiacs as much for its low cost as for its easy preparation.

Millet should be eaten more often. Unfortunately, most people see millet only as birdseed, although millions of people in Asia, Africa and Europe eat it daily. It has been cultivated for centuries in China, Russia, India and Europe, and more recently, in North America. This yellowish grain looks like a rounded sesame seed and is about one millimeter in diameter. The best quality millet has a golden color.

Besides containing as much or more protein than rice, corn and oats, it also surpasses other grains with a wide range of nutrients. These include calcium, iron, phosphorus, magnesium, manganese, potassium, silicone and B vitamins. Another important aspect of millet is that it is an alkaline grain and non-mucous forming. For this reason, it helps maintain acid-base balance in the body, which is often a dilemma when people are ill. Contrary to most grains, which are slightly acidifying, millet's alkaline nature contributes to better digestion. It rarely causes an allergic reaction to sensitive individuals, and is not irritating to nervous stomachs or more fragile digestive systems. Millet also helps to replenish normal bowel flora and eliminates constipation.

Millet can be prepared as hot cereal for breakfast, as an alternative to rice, added to soup, pancake and muffin recipes or as millet milk.

Preparation: Always start by washing millet carefully, rinsing it two or three times. If cooked as a grain, use 625 ml (2 ½ cups) of water per 250 ml (1 cup) millet. Bring both to a boil, then let simmer covered for 40 to 50 minutes. It is cooked when it is light and fluffy without sticking together. More water is necessary for the cereal than for the main-dish millet. Use 750 to 1000 ml (3 to 4 cups) of water per 250 ml (1 cup) millet and cook the same way but longer, 50 to 60 minutes. Dates or dried apricots can be added when almost cooked, if desired. One cup whole grain gives approximately 4 portions. Millet milk is made in the blender by mixing 250 ml (1 cup) cooked millet with 250 ml (1 cup) water or soymilk. A little vanilla or maple syrup may be added for taste. All you need to do when you want to use it is to shake it well. Some people cook millet throughout the night in a slow cooker to have it ready when they wake up.

Quinoa is considered a super grain because it is a powerhouse of nutrients and is easy to grow. It was one of the staple foods of the Inca civilization for centuries. They recognized its health benefits and encouraged pregnant and lactating women to eat quinoa more often. They called it "mother" or "mother grain". It is now cultivated in Canada.

Contrarily to other grains, quinoa contains all eight of the essential amino acids, making it a high quality protein similar to milk. By adding a few vegetables, it provides a complete and well-balanced meal. It is an excellent source of calcium, potassium, zinc, iron, magnesium and B vitamins as well as essential fatty acids. Its protein content is 16% compared to 7.5% for rice and 14 % for wheat. Quinoa also contains about the same amount of oxalic acid as spinach. Oxalates can cause some problems for sensitive individuals such as arthritics, but in general, when used in moderation, it is very well tolerated.

Quinoa seeds are endowed with a bitter coating of saponins that must be washed off before cooking. To remove the coating, wash the seeds 3 to 5 times in cold water, swishing well and draining in a strainer after each rinse. Continue rinsing quinoa until it does not produce much foam. Agronomists speculate that this coating helped the species to survive all this time by acting as a built-in pest deterrent. The saponins are not harmful but taste very bitter. For this reason, it is not possible to make your own flour from the seeds. Manufacturers have developed a system of belts against which the seeds are jostled, thus imitating the action of sandpaper. This takes away the saponins before grinding the seeds into flour.

Preparation: While keeping in mind that one cup of grain makes four cooked portions, we can use quinoa to make an excellent cereal. Measure 625 to 875 ml (2 1/2 to 3 1/2 cups) of water per 250 ml (1 cup) of quinoa. Bring to a boil, then simmer, covered for 15 to 30 minutes. To serve it as a rice substitute, use less water, 500 to 750 ml (2 to 3 cups) per 250 ml (1 cup) of quinoa. Cook quinoa until light and tasty; 15 to 25 minutes. Vegetables can be added during cooking or afterwards.

Brown rice is a favorite throughout the world and is the most popular grain after wheat. Rice constitutes about 50% of calorie intake for more than half of the world's population. It is still the main cereal culture in Asia, even though other countries are also important producers. Approximately 94% of world production is concentrated in the Orient. China, India, Indonesia, Bangladesh and Thailand are some of the greatest rice producing countries in the world. Rice culture thrives in tropical climates.

There are as many as 8000 varieties of rice. The whole grain rice is covered by a brown husk, which must be removed before human consumption. Brown rice, whether short or long, is the whole grain with this husk removed and the rest of the kernel intact, still containing the bran and germ. It is easily digestible while supplying a portion of protein equivalent to cheese, and slightly higher than that of red meat. Rice is a good source of magnesium, B6 vitamin, niacin, thiamine, phosphorus, zinc and copper, as well as containing traces of pantothenic acid and potassium. White rice has been husked and polished therefore losing a lot of nutrients. In some countries, white rice is enriched with iron, niacin and thiamine.

94

Wild rice deserves a mention if only for its rich nutty taste. As it is quite scarce, it is expensive, but it is also delicious and nutritious. A handful can be added to brown rice to enhance both taste and appearance. It is preferable to pre-soak wild rice ahead of time for an hour or two, or it can just be boiled for 10 minutes; this will reduce cooking time. Discard cooking water and cook it along with brown rice. Wild rice is a good source of complex carbohydrates while supplying protein and vitamins.

Preparation: Wash brown rice by rubbing it together with your hands, swishing it around to dislodge excess starch, dirt and stray rice husks. Repeat until water remains relatively clear. Using 500 to 625 ml (2 to 2 1/2 cups) water per 250 ml (1 cup) brown rice, bring to a boil on medium heat while covered, and then turn down to a low bubble for 45 minutes. White rice does not need to be rinsed and takes less time to cook. Vegetable broth can be added to the water for a different flavor. Diced vegetables or herbs can also be added during the last 15 to 20 minutes of cooking time. Do not stir while cooking or it will become sticky.

The Chinese cultivated buckwheat for hundreds of years. Traders exchanged it during their expeditions and that is how it traveled from Asia to Europe, and then to America. By the mid-1800's, before wheat and corn became so popular, buckwheat was an important crop in this country. Unfortunately, its cultivation seems to be regressing throughout the world. This cereal belongs to the same family as rhubarb and is not related to wheat or rye. It contains no gluten and is accepted in a gluten-free diet.

Buckwheat is rich in nutrients such as vitamins B, E and K, calcium, magnesium, iron, sulfur, phosphorus, sodium, potassium, zinc, manganese and copper. It contains almost as much protein as eggs but no cholesterol. It is a good source of rutin, which is a bioflavonoid that helps strengthen the walls of blood vessels, making it useful in case of hemorrhage, hemorrhoids and varicose veins. Buckwheat is usually well tolerated by individuals sensitive to wheat or gluten-grains. However some people with celiac disease cannot tolerate buckwheat because they are sensitive to its rutin fraction.

Buckwheat groats are the hulled, crushed kernels, which are usually cooked in a manner similar to rice. Groats come in coarse, medium and fine grinds. Kasha, which is roasted buckwheat groats, has a toasty, nutty flavor. The reddish color buckwheat has a stronger taste than the lighter colored one. Buckwheat comes in different forms such as buckwheat flakes, flour and even pasta. It can be used to make delicious cereal, waffles, pancakes or even cakes. This highly nutritious cereal deserves a place on your menu.

Preparation: Use about 500 ml (2 cups) water per 250 ml (1 cup) grain (buckwheat groats). Bring to a boil, and then turn heat down to a low bubble. Let it simmer, covered, for 20 to 30 minutes until no longer crunchy, adding extra water if needed. Onions, herbs or salt can be added at the end of cooking time (last 5 - 10 minutes). Cook kasha the same way, but with a bit less water and reducing cooking time to 15 to 20 minutes.

Though **soya** (also spelled soy) is not a cereal or a grain, but rather a legume, it has become such a versatile food nowadays, that it is well worth mentioning. The soya bean originated from Asia and is a greatly appreciated food in the Far East. It can be prepared as any other member of the legume family, though it takes a bit longer to cook than most beans. Soya beans are nourishing since they are protein-rich.

Most people will argue that tofu is a food of modern times, yet, in China, it has been valued for more than 2000 years. Tofu is made from a milky liquid extracted from soybeans. It has a gelatinous consistence, and it is found in stores in the shape of rectangular blocks, available in different degrees of firmness, depending on whether it is meant as a meat substitute or as an ingredient for a creamy dessert. As tofu is rather flavorless on its own, it easily takes in the taste of the foods it is cooked with.

Two hundred and fifty grams (8 ounces) of tofu provides 164 calories, 17, 6 grams of protein, 292 milligrams of calcium (the same as 8 ounces of milk), 286 milligrams of phosphorus, and as much iron as 4 to 5 eggs.[2] Tofu keeps well in the refrigerator, covered in water in a close container; just rinse and change the water each day.

Soya provides a complete protein, as well as essential fatty acids including linolenic acid also called omega-3. Soya beans contain calcium, iron, potassium, B vitamins and lecithin. Sprouting soya beans increases its nutritive value many times over. Soya is available as flour, milk, yogurt and ice cream. It is also the main ingredient in soya cheese, miso, tempeh and tamari sauce. Soya is praised for the numerous health benefits it seems to provide, from relief of menopause discomfort, to the prevention of cholesterol, heart disease and even cancer.

When soya is first introduced in the diet, it necessitates the same precautions as corn since it is also a potentially allergenic food. Soya, the new ancient food, can add variety to your meals, whether as soya cheese at breakfast or in the spaghetti sauce at supper; it offers a wide range of choices, limited only by your imagination.

Teff is an ancient, recently rediscovered grain with a nutty taste. Genetically, it is closer to rice and corn than to wheat. It is now accepted by the American Dietetic Association (ADA) as a gluten-free grain, and has been included in the 6th edition of the Manual of Clinical Dietetics. Doctors currently use this manual as a guide to the dietary treatment of various illnesses.

Teff has traveled to the United States from Ethiopia via Wayne Carlson, a Peace Corp worker. He realized the importance of teff to the people of this country while working there in the early 1970's. As he had grown accustomed to its taste, he missed it when he returned home. Since he needed a job, he decided to try raising teff at home, in Idaho, near the Oregon border. For the first five years, he supplied teff to Ethiopian restaurants in many American cities. Encouraged by an enthusiastic response from restaurant owners, he kept producing more and more, until he finally entered the health food market in 1988.

The word teff means "lost ". It is a minuscule little seed, even smaller that amaranth. It is surprisingly wholesome. Besides being a good source of protein, it is 5 times richer in iron, calcium and potassium that any other grain. Teff grows in many varieties; it comes in ivory, brown and reddish tan, although the brown kind sells better. Teff seeds can be cooked as cereal or its flour added to recipes.

Preparation: Rinse the seeds well until water remains clear. It needs more water than other grains to cook, so use four times more water than seeds. Simmer for 15 to 20 minutes, covered, until all the water is absorbed.

Less common grains or starches can also enhance a gluten-free diet and make eating more exciting. **Sorghum**, a distant relative to corn, is utilized for human consumption to make flour and beverages. Many populations in Africa and India have consumed sorghum for thousands of years. It is now widely found in the drier areas of Africa, Asia, the Americas and Australia.

Manioc, also called cassava or yucca, originated from Brazil and Central America. It was an essential food for the Indians of Brazil for decades. Its large, tuberous roots, which are rich in starch, are the source of tapioca and Brazilian arrowroot. Manioc can be used to make cakes or flat breads.

Arrowroot, different from the Brazilian arrowroot, is also named Indian arrowroot or maranta. It is found mostly in the warm, swampy forests of Central and South America. It makes an easily digestible starch used mostly as a thickening agent just as cornstarch.

African millet, also known as coracana millet or ragi, is an important food crop in Eastern Africa, Asia, India and Nepal. Its seed is smaller than other varieties of millet, measuring about one to two millimeters in diameter.

Job's tear, also referred to as Coix lacryma-jobi or Christ's tear, is a tear shaped grain. Job's tear is also commonly known as Chinese pearl barley in America. After cooking (which requires an hour or more), it does taste like the common barley though it does not contain gluten. It is a secondary cereal cultivated in South Eastern Asia.

Sago is a starch extracted from the sago palms. It is processed into flour, meal and pearl sago, which is similar to tapioca. South Pacific cooks frequently use sago for baking and for thickening soups, puddings and other desserts. In the Orient and in India, it is mostly used as flour while in the United States it occasionally serves as a thickening agent.

In an article entitle *How to manage common food allergies and retain your sanity*, published in the magazine *Health Naturally* of June/July 1998, Carola Barczak, well recognized in the field of natural health, proposed substitutes to wheat flour. As an alternative to 250 ml (one cup) of wheat flour, she suggested: 150 ml (10 tablespoons) potato flour; 200 ml (14 tablespoons) rice flour; 125 ml rice flour (½ cup) plus 80 ml (1/3 cup) potato flour; or 250 ml (1 cup) soy flour plus 125 ml (½ cup) potato flour. To pre-mix an all-purpose flour substitute that can be used for just about anything except bread, thoroughly blend 180 ml (¾ cup) potato flour, 60 ml (¼ cup) soy flour, 500 ml (2 cups) rice flour and 60 ml (4 tablespoons) each arrowroot powder and tapioca flour. She added that flour combinations require at least six siftings and long, slower baking at a lower temperature. She also recommended 10 ml (2 teaspoons) of baking powder for each cup or 250 ml of flour. For thickening gravy, she replaces wheat flour with half the amount of arrowroot.

The benefits of breastfeeding

In view of the fact that this chapter is dedicated to food, we have to include a few words about breastfeeding. Doctors, nurses and mothers have enthusiastically discussed the wonderful benefits of breast milk on a child's health many times over. Many studies have been done to find out whether breastfeeding a baby can trigger celiac disease or protect against it. We know that to develop the disease, the child must have a celiac gene, contributed by one or both of his parents.

A study by Auricchio concluded that babies fed with commercial formulas or breastfed for less than one month had four times more chances of developing symptoms of celiac disease than infants breastfed for more than a month.[3]

In the book *Breastfeeding and Human Lactation* (2nd edition), many studies cited demonstrate that artificial milk and early introduction of solid foods can accelerate the development of symptoms of celiac disease.[4] This could explain why the incidence of celiac disease has diminished since breastfeeding made a big comeback and by the fact that solid foods are introduced later. Generally, a celiac child that has no antecedent of celiac disease in the family history should thrive normally and should not demonstrate any symptoms until solid gluten-containing foods are introduced.

Another study pointed out that prolonged breastfeeding for a period of six months or more and a late introduction of gluten, after the age of five months, could considerably delay the emergence of celiac's symptoms. The introduction of gluten in an infant's diet should be done progressively and while breastfeeding is ongoing to insure more protection. They believed that adding gluten to the diet two months before weaning has a protective effect.[5]

The question of whether or not nursing mothers can pass gluten through breast milk has been debated for years. It has now been verified that gliadin, the gluten protein, does circulate through breast milk. It would follow that gliadin should reach the child's bloodstream, but this part of the statement is still hypothetic and necessitates more studies.

According to Dr. Karoly Horvath, one of the directors of the celiac center at the University of Maryland in Baltimore: "Breast milk contains antibodies against all the antigens the mother's immune system has met prior to or during pregnancy and has produced antibodies to them. This is the way that mother's milk protects babies from all the antigens (infectious agents, toxins, allergens…) occurring in the environment where the mother lives. Without this protection, the antigens may enter the body through the digestive or respiratory systems. The best example is that breast milk protects babies from bacteria causing diarrhea in underdeveloped countries. In brief, breast milk may contain all the antibodies the mother has in her digestive and respiratory systems. The function of these antibodies is to block the entrance of antigens to the baby's digestive and respiratory systems."

Dr. Horvath adds that in the case of celiac disease, if the mother has circulating antibodies to gliadin, these antibodies will appear in the milk. If the breast-fed baby ingests gliadin (if the mother inadvertently ingested gluten and traces of gliadin appear in the milk), the antibodies in the milk will block the gliadin and it will not be able to cross the intestinal wall to meet the baby' immune system. Theoretically, the breast-fed infant does not have any immunoreactions to gliadin. If the mother accidentally ingests gliadin during breast-feeding, it is likely that the concentration of antigliadin antibodies will increase in the breast milk. In conclusion, the antibodies in breast milk are protective and do not trigger celiac disease in genetically predisposed babies. Furthermore, it is well documented that breast-feeding in the first year of life decreases the risk of allergies by 50% in babies whose parents have allergies.»[6]

The book *Breastfeeding: A Guide for the Medical Profession* mentions an interesting study by Troncone and his colleagues. They measured how much time was needed before gliadin was found in breast milk after the ingestion of 20 grams of the gluten protein. Gliadin was found in the milk of 54 of the 80 mothers within two to four hours after its intake, but it never appeared in the baby's blood. The authors concluded that the gliadin transfer from the mother to the baby was essential to establish an immune response in the child. The epidemiologic data suggest considering breastfeeding especially appropriate in families with celiac antecedents.[7]

Much more research will be needed to study every aspect of breastfeeding with regard to celiac disease. In the meantime, if there is reason to suspect celiac disease because it runs in the family, the nursing mother should avoid gluten until the baby has been weaned. There are also gluten-free formulas available. In spite of all the unanswered questions surrounding this dilemma, breastfeeding offers too many benefits to pass up this wonderful and natural gesture.

CHAPTER SIX

Other sources of gluten

You probably think you know every single source of gluten by now. Surprise! Gluten hides in the most sneaky and unexpected places. Celiacs must become experts at detecting the enemy. We must be on alert at all times as things change very quickly. There is a continual need for vigilance; we must beware and investigate all new foods, and be particularly sharp-eyed when labels on products used regularly mention "new and improved". This is where an in-depth knowledge of glutinous ingredients becomes essential. When in doubt, do not hesitate to review the list of forbidden ingredients. Keep it handy; make several copies, place one on the refrigerator door, another in your handbag, and pass them out to friends and family.

If all the maneuvering to avoid gluten were limited to the food portion of our existence, the challenge would already be significant. Unfortunately, gluten is so polyvalent that it is used as an unsuspected ingredient in many different contexts. This chapter is dedicated to uncovering some of these hidden situations.

Alcohol beverages and gluten

Alcohol contributes to food allergies in many ways. It increases the permeability of the intestinal lining therefore permitting allergenic substances to be absorbed in the bloodstream resulting in allergic reactions. This makes alcohol an important factor to consider in regard to the "leaky gut" syndrome.

The stomach and the intestine absorb alcohol very quickly. A rapid absorption combined with the fact that one could also react to an ingredient in the beverage, can turn an alcoholic drink into powerful allergen. This allergenic aspect is what makes it a powerful addictant, as observed in the case of alcoholism. Clinical studies showed that social drinkers who become inebriated on as little as two servings of beer or whisky were found to be sensitive to corn, wheat, malt, barley, rye or yeast.

Let's re-examine this situation while applying it to a gluten intolerant individual. A person with celiac disease will most likely have an increased intestinal permeability and we know without a doubt that this person does not tolerated some of the ingredients mentioned above. Following this line of thinking, we can conclude that gluten intolerant people may be hypersensitive to alcoholic beverages. They either become inebriated faster than most or they may have physical or mental symptoms such as abdominal pain or even an unjustified feeling of sadness or anxiety. This reaction to the gluten in the beverage may be exaggerated or more intense than the usual reaction to gluten, due to the fact that alcohol speeds up the absorption process.

Corn, barley, rye, oats, wheat and rice are the common grains used in the production of whisky and vodka. The first three are usually used to make gin, while corn and barley are necessary to the production of beer and ale. Other ingredients found in alcoholic beverages are sugar cane, malt or yeast.

An issue often brought up by celiacs is whether they can consume alcohol beverages, and if so, which ones. While excluding immoderation, several alcoholic beverages are now permitted in the gluten-free diet. It is important to take into account other food allergies; for example, some wines contain sulphites and must be avoided by sensitive individuals. Then again, if drinking even a small quantity of alcohol brings about unpleasant symptoms, good sense dictates abstinence. A person recently diagnosed with celiac disease should definitely wait until the intestine recovers a bit of vitality before exposing it to a harsh irritant such as alcohol.

The Canadian Celiac Association Handbook states that: "Beer and ale, usually made from barley, may contain 1-2 mg of prolamins per pint

(570mL) and therefore is not allowed. Wines are made from grapes and are allowed. Fortified wines such as sherry and port contain added alcohol and are also allowed. Distilled alcoholic beverages such as gin, vodka, Scotch whisky and rye whisky are made from the fermentation of wheat, barley or rye. Since they are distilled, they do not contain prolamins and are allowed unless otherwise contraindicated."[1]

Controversy about alcohol has been going on for a long time. Some celiac associations are more permissive than others, and this creates a lot of confusion for people who would enjoy adding an occasional alcoholic treat to their gluten-free diet. It is only recently that the American Dietetic Association (ADA) has released the 6th edition of its *Manual of Clinical Dietetics*, which offers revised guidelines for the treatment of celiac disease. This manual is currently used by hospitals and doctors all over North America as the most up-to-date source of information with regard to the dietary treatment of various illnesses. The new values set in this publication conform more closely with current international standards. The new guidelines are another step towards the ultimate goal to set an international standard for all celiac organizations in the world. For the first time, the United States and Canada have united their gluten-free standards. Now included in their safe list are: amaranth, buckwheat, distilled vinegar (no matter what its source), distilled alcoholic beverages (including rum, whiskey and vodka), millet, quinoa and teff.[2]

Nowadays, there is a spectacular diversity of alcoholic beverages, so one must be aware that other gluten containing ingredients could be added. It is often the case for some liqueurs and coolers. Beer drinkers do not despair; there is now beer made from buckwheat or sorghum available. As many alcoholic beverages are not labeled with a precise ingredient list, one must always be careful. As the quote says: "When you doubt, abstain."

Medication

It is three o'clock in the morning; you are feeling sick and feverish. You reach for the medicine chest and take the first fever-reducing medicine you can find. Of course, nothing is that easy for celiacs.

Medication is another concealed source of gluten. Often, even if in very small quantities, gluten can be part of a pill's coating, or part of its active principal. Gluten is found in medication under many different names such as wheat starch (beware of starch with no specified source), wheat germ oil, wheat bran, barley bran, vegetable amylase (barley) and alpha-amylase (barley), or also in the form of stabilizers, fillers, flavors and other ingredients.

Ask your doctor's help when you need a prescription, and verify all the ingredients included in the medication with the pharmacist, explaining that you suffer from celiac disease and must avoid all gluten. For medication taken directly from the shelves, once again, turn to your pharmacist for reassurance. If you do not get a clear answer and still have doubts about a remedy, do not hesitate to consult another expert. Since celiac disease is still fairly unknown, we must continue to demand that our particular needs be met by asking questions repeatedly if necessary; that is the only way the health community will finally be informed that gluten intolerance does exist. Another way to get information is to contact the company responsible for making the medication. This may require a bit of time and patience, but you will at least be reassured that your medicine is truly gluten-free. Do not forget to use the same cautious approach for all natural products even if it is only a vitamin supplement. Laxatives demand the same attention. Vigilance is a must since buying medication is not something we do often and the formula can change from one time to the next.

Hidden risks

The hospital is where we go when we need medical care. Who would have thought that hospitalization or even an outpatient visit for a checkup could entail a health risk? Nevertheless, this is really the case for an unadvised celiac.

To start with, every gluten intolerant individual should designate a reliable person who will be responsible for transmitting the celiac diagnosis to the medical staff in the event he is unable to do so himself, as in the case of an accident or the need for immediate surgery. This may seem like a drastic measure, but did you ever consider what would happen if you were involved in a situation of this kind? It is worthwhile taking certain precautions.

If a hospitalization is planned ahead of time, it will be easier to advise the dietary department of your special needs. You can also ask a family member or a friend to bring in special gluten-free meals from home. Upon arrival, inform all concerned nursing staff (doctors, nurses, dietician) responsible for your care of your particular gluten-free requirements. Remember to inform all new doctors you consult with, as they may not have your whole medical history at hand.

Some medical tests also demand cautiousness. Barium used for a barium meal and enema may contain gluten. If you have any procedures involving dyes, be sure to remind your doctor and the technician that you have celiac disease and may be dangerously sensitive to dye solutions. Do not trust that since they work in a hospital, they know what to check for; with so many patients every day, they need all the help we can provide, and in this case, your life may depend on it.

Who would have thought that Play Doh could constitute a health risk? Once again, celiacs must think of everything. Though gluten cannot be absorbed through the skin, young children like to taste things, so this eye-catching multicolored Play Doh, which often contains gluten, could well end up in the mouth. The same applies to glue, play clay and papier mâché. Many of these craft products can be homemade with gluten-free ingredients and some recipes are even edible.

Since communion wafers also contain gluten, this is another source of frustration for some people. Certain companies now make gluten-free wafers. Just ask your priest, minister or pastor about how a gluten-free wafer may be hosted.

Additional things to beware of are licking envelopes, stamps or other gummed labels, which may have gluten-containing glue.

Blood donation

A non-negligible aspect of celiac disease is the privilege to give blood. When asked this question, Hema-Quebec responded as follows: "If celiac disease is well controlled by a gluten-free diet, the person will be accepted for a blood donation. If the individual shows symptoms of the disease, he or she must wait twelve months after the last symptoms before giving blood."

This statement brings out some interesting points. How can we be sure that the gluten-free diet is respected at 100% even with the best of intentions? Gluten tends to hide everywhere and a dietary error can take place unknowingly. Some people have atypical symptoms such as migraine and depression. How is it possible to ascertain that gluten is or is not at cause? We must conclude that giving blood is a very personal issue, which depends on one's own beliefs, and that it is simply ethically correct to advise the medical personnel of our celiac condition before we give blood.

Skin care

Certain brands of shampoos and lotions contain wheat or a derivative. This prompts us to ask the following question: "Can gluten be absorbed through the skin? " According to Dr. John Zone, a dermatologist who is an expert on dermatitis herpetiformis, the answer is no. Gluten that is present in topically applied make-ups and lotions is not absorbed because the protein molecules in gluten are too large. Most brands of toothpaste are gluten-free, but it's a good idea to check with the manufacturer to make sure there aren't any hidden sources of gluten.[3]

According to an article entitled *Products for patients with special needs*", for some celiacs, likely less than three to five percent of the celiac population, there may be an additional concern related to selected ingredients such as soaps, cosmetics and detergents applied to the skin. And, there are those "highly sensitive" individuals who must be careful regarding a sensitivity, reaction or toxicity to odors and elements breathed into the lungs and therefore absorbed through capillary action. There seems to be little research literature regarding reaction to topical application.

The following research examples have been reported. Some reactions can be brought on by another ingredient in cosmetics, creams and lotions, such as alcohol, selected polymers, dyes and preservatives. As celiacs are less tolerant in general, this could explain some of the negative effects. Common items which can cause adverse reactions include lipsticks containing oat gum, hair sprays, eye shadow mixes, perfumes, soaps and shampoos, which may contain dye, alcohol-based scents, or even wheat germ oil. People diagnosed with dermatitis herpetiformis, young children or older celiacs are more sensitive and this may be because their immune systems are less resistant.[4]

Non-allergenic soaps, detergents, shampoos and a large variety of cosmetics are available at most drugstores.

Cross-contamination

In a previous chapter, we discussed cross-contamination with regard to oats. Let us now investigate other points of view. As we tackle the subject of cross-contamination, we are faced yet again with controversy. How can you be certain that your flour has been ground in a gluten-free environment, that the equipment was thoroughly cleaned before use, or that air-borne gluten flour in the bakery did not contaminate your rice flour cookies? As you can see, a celiac has to make a decision. The individual can either live in fear of gluten to the point of staying awake at night, or can choose do be as diligent as possible in making gluten-free choices, accepting that 100% effort may result in 98% success, while permitting some peace of mind. It is much more reasonable to do one's best to steer clear of the dreaded protein, and to avoid turning the situation into a phobic and obsessive drama. The best way to attain this level of acceptation is certainly information. When there is light, darkness disappears, and when we examine a situation with a clear mind, fear often fades away.

Here is a list of precautions that will quickly become part of your everyday routine:

Celiacs should have their own butter dish, cutting board, toaster, and if possible, a specific corner of the kitchen counter. These precautions ensure that gluten-containing breadcrumbs won't end up in the gluten-free food.

If making two kinds of pasta, have an extra colander at hand or drain the gluten-free pasta first. Do not use the same utensils to stir gluten-free and gluten-containing pasta.

Use a clean utensil each time you reach into a jar (peanut butter, jam). If a knife used to butter a piece of whole wheat toast finds its way into the peanut butter, be assured that some crumbs are left behind in the jar. It is a habit the whole family will have to get used to. Once a utensil has gone into a jar, it will not be used again. For everyday items like butter, jam and peanut butter, it is sometimes easier just to buy two of everything and mark it with a marker. Beware of visitors that don't yet know the celiac way!

When preparing food, get in the habit of making the gluten-free version first. It will prevent airborne flour from landing in your gluten-free preparation. Be sure to use a different sifter for each kind of flour. A small percentage of celiacs are so sensitive that even breathing in gluten-containing flour can cause some problems, as the flour will end up being absorbed in the system.

At the health food store and the grocery store, beware of cross-contamination between bulk bins selling flours and grains. The scoops could have also been used in a gluten-containing bin. Many stores avoid this problem by attaching a scoop to each bin with a rope or small chain.

Grilled or fried food at the restaurant could have been cooked in a gluten-contaminated environment (grill, frying oil); for example, French fries fried in the same cooking oil as onions rings.

This list does not pretend to cover all situations. Its goal is to give you a few guidelines. Once you catch on to the general idea, time and practice will do the rest. Your way of seeing the world will broaden and your mind will soon include a gluten-free sphere. It is all right to make a mistake once in a while; grant yourself permission not to understand everything immediately. There is no shame to feeling discouraged, even enraged with the diagnosis, whether it is yours or that of a close relative. Seeing an improvement in your health or that of a loved one will be your biggest reward for your patience and willingness to learn. By then, you will have a better comprehension of celiac disease, and this will encourage you to pursue your adventure with food. Support groups are available and offer precious and much appreciated help in times of uncertainty. Lean on them when you feel the need for comfort and new ideas.

CHAPTER SEVEN

Recovering our health

For all living inhabitants of this world, whether human or animal, the need for food for survival is predominant. Unfortunately, the basis of good nutrition itself is frequently forgotten to profit the food industry. The consumer becomes, consciously or not, the victim of a frantic lifestyle, led to make fast-food choices, and encouraged to select foods for its seductive wrapping instead of its nutritional value. A large part of our population nourish themselves inadequately; our bodies are overfed with refined, preservative flavored foods, while our immune systems are starving for essential nutrients. Long-term abuse of this kind leads to a weakening of the immune system paving the way to a variety of illnesses.

The diet

When one suffers from a condition such as celiac disease, the importance of good nutrition becomes crucial. Although dietetic restrictions for celiacs are numerous, their choices are often healthier than the average population. Having to decipher each ingredient on a label gives us the opportunity to make intelligent and nutritive choices. Nutrition is the relationship between food and our physical wellbeing; it is, in fact, the combination of transformations and utilization our body makes of the food to ensure its growth and activities.

Many people mistakenly believe that excluding gluten foods will automatically lead to nutritional deficiencies. On the contrary, once a strict gluten-free diet is started, the inflammation will begin to subside, usually within a few weeks. Significant healing and regrowth of the villi in the small intestine will take place, and food absorption will soon be back to full capacity. Food choices than become very important to help restore deficient vitamins and minerals necessary to good health.

Naturally, a well-balanced gluten-free diet will simultaneously promote healing of the bowel lining and provide the missing nutrients. The first step is to substitute the prohibited grains with gluten-free starches and grains, which are an invaluable source of essential nutrients, as seen in chapter 5.

Permitted foods include meat, poultry, fish and seafood, fruits and vegetables, gluten-free grains and cereals, eggs, legumes, nuts (almond, hazelnut, cashew…), seeds (sunflower, pumpkin, sesame…), as well as cold-pressed oils which contain essential fatty acids. Dairy products can be included according to one's individual level of tolerance to lactose. As mentioned earlier in the book, lactose intolerance sometimes disappears after a person has followed a gluten-free diet long enough for the intestinal healing process to begin. When you reintroduce dairy products, be attentive to intolerance symptoms such as bloating, stomach pain and diarrhea. Soya milk is a pleasant substitute to cow's milk, but avoid flavored varieties that often contain barley malt.

Since celiac disease is an autoimmune disease, it goes without saying that any food or drink detrimental to the immune system should be avoided or consumed very moderately. Healing or recovery of any kind necessitates the elimination of harmful foods, the addition of essential nutritional elements, as well as a reduction of acidic residue in the body and a reasonable period of time to recuperate. Products such as sugar and its derivatives, coffee, tea, soft drinks, alcoholic beverages are irritant and acidifying to the human body and provide no nutritional benefits.

If one cheats

In view of the complexity of the gluten-free regime, one can inadvertently consume a small amount of gluten, especially on trips away from home. There is no easy solution except to wait out the symptoms.

Some people claim that various enzymes can assist in the breakdown of gluten, and can therefore be helpful to celiacs who accidentally or even intentionally ingest gluten. Dr. Joseph A. Murray of the Mayo Clinic does not recommend such enzymes. He says: "There is no evidence that it will prevent the damaging effects of gluten in people with celiac disease. It is unlikely that it would be so efficient as to get rid of all the gluten that has been swallowed. I would not recommend it as a treatment for celiac disease."[1]

A strict gluten-free diet, though challenging, is the only treatment known to date for celiac disease. Several reports indicate that 60 to 70 percent of celiac patients handle the imposed diet very well and see it as an opportunity to manage the disease positively. This category of individuals has fewer related and non-related health problems. Regrettably, many celiacs, either because they are not convinced of the need of such a strict regime, by lack of knowledge about the diet and the disease, by lack of motivation, or even by deliberate choice, decide not to respect these stringent dietary rules. There are also those celiacs who may choose to cheat now and then, often doing so for as long as their symptoms are bearable and don't interfere too much with their lives. Unfortunately, 30 to 40 percent of celiacs belong to this group, putting themselves at risk for long-term consequences. We will not review the implications brought on by these choices since we have discussed the incurred risks repeatedly throughout the book.

Some articles on celiac disease mention the risk of anaphylactic shock when wheat is reintroduce accidentally. Anaphylactic shock is a life threatening form of allergic reaction potentially fatal if not treated immediately. It can be caused by a reaction to a food, or a severe response to a medication or insect sting. Vast quantities of histamine are released throughout the body causing rapid swelling and breathing difficulty that can lead to a collapse of the circulatory system, of which a sudden drop of blood pressure is a symptom, and even to convulsions. An allergic reaction to wheat is an immunologic reaction against a fraction of the wheat, whether it is gliadin, glutenin or another. The reaction is usually immediate or in the hour that follows ingestion. It is always possible for a diagnosed celiac to be also allergic to wheat, but this fact would most likely have been discovered at an earlier time, and the individual would be well prepared. People at risk for anaphylactic shock usually carry an adrenaline syringe with them at all times. Besides, an allergic reaction to wheat is rarely this severe.

It is important to recognize that gluten intolerance is not an allergy. Celiac disease is an intolerance to the wheat protein called gliadin, and although its symptoms can be unpleasant, it does not imply potentially fatal short-term danger such as an anaphylactic shock represents. It is crucial to be well informed to avoid panic amongst newly diagnosed sufferers, especially if they are children that depend on their parents for guidance and reassurance.

Avoiding nutrient deficiencies

Since every disease related to the intestine also implicates a lack of assimilation of essential nutrients, it is important that the treatment involves a dietary plan to fill those needs. Celiac disease primarily affects the upper part of the small intestine, and depending on the severity of the condition, it can eventually progress to the jejunum and even to the lower part the small bowel called the ileum. As the absorption of most nutrients takes place in the small intestine, it is important to rectify the situation as quickly as possible. Depletion of essential nutrients can lead to numerous health problems. Adding nutritional supplements to a gluten-free diet can accelerate the intestinal healing process and the return of good health. The following pages review the basics of nutrition to help you understand how to fulfill your nutritional deficiencies.

Carbohydrates

Dietary carbohydrates consist of starch, sugar and fiber. They are the primary source of energy for all bodily functions, while proteins are used for building and repairing tissue. Carbohydrates are important in the metabolism of fat, and the digestion and absorption

116

of other foods. When the jejunum is damaged, all forms of carbohydrates may be poorly absorbed.

A deficiency of carbohydrates can lead to a lack of energy, concentration problems, depression, weight loss and acidosis. An excess of carbohydrates can cause obesity and digestive disturbances.

Sources of starches, or complex carbohydrates, include fruits, vegetables, dried beans, grains and cereals. Simple carbohydrates, or sugars, include table sugar, honey, natural fruit sugars and molasses. These must be consumed very moderately.

Proteins
Proteins are essential to the growth and development of all body tissues of which they constitute the main building material (refer to the beginning of chapter 3). Proteins are also used in the formation of antibodies.

A protein deficiency can lead to a lack of vitality and endurance, muscle wasting, growth retardation, depression, as well as a weak resistance to infection. An exaggerated excess of protein can be harmful to the kidneys and can contribute to obesity.

Sources of proteins include meat, fish, seafood, fowl, eggs, dairy products, whole grains, nuts, legumes and tofu.

Fats
Fats are organic compounds that are insoluble in water but soluble in other fats or lipids. They contribute to the absorption of fat-soluble vitamins (A, D, E and K) in the intestines. The body needs fuel to function and fats offer the most concentrated source of food energy. As the body's energy provider, they help the body maintain a constant temperature. Fats play a role in maintaining nerve impulse transmission and memory storage. Fat deposits also help to

insulate the body and to support and protect various organs against bumping and rubbing.

Fats are divided into three categories: saturated, monounsaturated and polyunsaturated. Saturated fats are usually solid at room temperature; the only sources of naturally saturated fat in our diet are animal fats and tropical oils (coconut, palm, cocoa butter). They should be consumed moderately as they seem to increase blood cholesterol.

Unsaturated fats are usually liquid at room temperature and include most vegetable oils. They are subdivided into monounsaturated fats (vegetable and nut oils – olive, canola, sesame, almond and peanut) and polyunsaturated fats (cold water fish, flax seed, seeds, nuts and grains). Unsaturated fats are healthier than saturated fats. They seem to raise the "good" cholesterol without increasing total cholesterol levels. Once oil is heated, it produces free radicals, so it is always preferable to use raw oils. Unsaturated fat liberates nine calories per gram, that is to say, 100 to 200 calories per tablespoon. Fat digestion is slow and could take from eight to nine hours. No more than 20 to 30% of our diet should consist of fats.

Hydrogenated fats (shortening, vegetable margarine) can cause a lot of damage to our health and should be avoided by everyone. Hydrogenation is a process that hardens liquid vegetable oils. It is found in ice cream, chocolate, potato chips and commercially prepared baked goods.

As most celiacs have trouble with fat absorption, it becomes an important aspect of dietary management. Fat malabsorption produces a bowel movement that is pale in color, voluminous and foul smelling. The stool sometimes floats and leaves an oily film on the surface of the water. A lipid deficiency can lead to a lack of essential fatty acids. It is necessary to distinguish which are the good sources of fats, as an excess of saturated fats in the diet is associated with heart disease, obesity, diabetes and cancer.

Essential fatty acids

Nowadays, the terms "essential fatty acid" or "EFA" are often heard or read about. As the name itself indicates, they are essential to good health, but we can only get them from food, as our body does not have the necessary components to synthesize them. Unsaturated fats provide the essential fatty acids the body needs. Our diet should include an equal amount of monounsaturated and polyunsaturated fats. Essential fatty acids participate in the production of prostaglandins, which are hormone-like substances implicated in blood circulation and anti-inflammatory response. They promote blood circulation by preventing the aggregation of blood platelets (blood components that form clots), and by facilitating the anti-inflammatory process (injury, allergies). They also stimulate the secretion of adrenal hormones, and play an important role for the skin and nervous system. These essential fatty acids can be obtained from cold-pressed virgin oils:

Alpha-linolenic acid (omega-3): flax (best source), sunflower and pumpkin seeds, salmon and tuna oils.

Linoleic acid (omega 6): safflower (best source), hemp, primrose and sunflower oils, hazelnut, almond, pecan and cashew nuts.

Since every cell in the human body needs essential fatty acids to maintain optimal health, a deficiency could result in a variety of problems. The following conditions or symptoms could benefit from a supplementation of essential fatty acids: skin problems (itchiness, dry skin, acne, eczema, psoriasis), susceptibility to infections, sterility in men, miscarriage in women, painful and/or inflammatory conditions (arthritis, painful joints), cardiac and circulatory problems including hypercholesterolemia, hypertension, premenstrual syndrome and painful periods, symptoms related to menopause (hot flashed, vaginal dryness), mental deterioration (confusion, chronic fatigue, schizophrenia), troubles related to anxiety and nervousness, attention deficit with or without hyperactivity, wounds that do not heal properly, alopecia (hair loss).

Although the population in general can benefit from a daily intake of essential fatty acids, it is more than evident that all people suffering from a disease or condition, which limits fat absorption, should immediately add these indispensable fats to their diets. Many brands of essential fatty acids add vitamin E to their formula to reduce the chance of altering the essential fatty acids by oxidation. Several months can pass before health benefits are noticed, but repair and healing inside the body are surely on their way much before that.

Vitamins

A vitamin is a substance that is vital to the well-being and proper functioning of the human body. Vitamins have an important role in transforming our food into energy. They protect us and reinforce every organ of our body. Vitamins are divided into two categories: the fat-soluble vitamins A, D, E, F (essential fatty acids) and K require the presence of fat carriers to be absorbed and the water-soluble vitamins, vitamin C, bioflavonoids and the B vitamins, including choline and inositol, dissolve in water.

Malabsorption of vitamins A, D, E and K can occur when the small intestine is damaged. As celiac disease often destroys the villi in both the jejunum and duodenum, which can lead to fat malabsorption, and since fat-soluble vitamins necessitate the presence of fat carriers to be absorbed, the celiac individual can be confronted with an aggravated case of fat malabsorption. Steatorrhea is the most visible sign of this problem. Let us continue by briefly exploring each vitamin, including the role it plays in our body, the signs and symptoms of deficiency, and a list of food sources to help replenish each nutrient.

Fat-soluble vitamins

Vitamin A

Functions: Growth and body repair (bones and teeth), essential for good eyesight, development and renewal of skin and mucous membranes (throat, nose, lungs, intestines), necessary for protein digestion and helps fight infection.

Signs and symptoms of deficiencies: Allergies, loss of appetite, sinusitis, lack of resistance to infection, eyesight problems, night blindness, cancer and tinnitus.

Food sources: Fish liver oil (halibut and cod), liver, dairy products, butter, egg yolk, yellow fruits (nectarine, peach, fig, apricot…), leafy green and yellow vegetables (carrot, sweet potato, squash, spinach…), alfalfa and dandelion.

Vitamin D

Functions: Bone growth and renewal as it stimulates the absorption of calcium and phosphorus, required for nervous system function and blood clotting, increases immunity and promotes skin health.

Signs and symptoms of deficiencies: Sensation of burning in mouth and throat, diarrhea, insomnia, myopia, nervousness, softening of bone (osteomalacia, osteoporosis, rickets) and teeth, and vulnerability to infection.

Food sources: Sunlight, fish oil, chicken liver, egg yolks, sardines in oil, mushrooms, dairy products and sunflower seeds.

Vitamin E

Functions: Anti-sterility and anti-abortive vitamin, prevents scarring, protects the body from the effects of pollution, free radicals and other toxins, helps prevent premature aging, cancer and other degenerative diseases, prevents cardiovascular troubles by its anticoagulant activity, good to muscles and nerves, diminishes hot flashes during menopause and is considered an anti-wriggle vitamin.

Signs and symptoms of deficiencies: Dry and lifeless hair, hair loss, miscarriage, sterility, reduced immune functions, cardiovascular diseases and neurological problems.

Food sources: Alfalfa, leafy green vegetables, cold-pressed safflower oil, eggs, nuts, almonds, sunflower seeds, bananas, carrots, tomatoes, dandelion leaves, watercress, soya beans, avocados, chicken, haddock and seaweeds.

Vitamin K
Functions: Essential to blood clotting (in case of hemorrhage, nosebleed), reduces excessive menstrual flow.

Signs and symptoms of deficiencies: Contusions, diarrhea, hemorrhage, miscarriage, painful or irregular menstruations and nosebleed.

Food sources: Leafy green vegetables (spinach), cold-pressed vegetable oils, goat's milk, most plants, alfalfa, soya beans, tomatoes, cauliflower, cabbage, carrots, potatoes and egg yolks. A healthy intestine manufactures vitamin K with the help of the intestinal friendly bacteria.

Water-soluble vitamins

B-complex vitamins
Functions: Act as stabilizers for the nervous system (premenstrual syndrome, anxiety, depression), work as coenzymes, helping enzymes carry out their functions, especially in the metabolism of carbohydrates, fats and proteins, important for cell reproduction (white and red cells production), promote healing, influence dream memory, generally indispensable to good bodily function.

Signs and symptoms of deficiencies: Depression, insomnia, lack of concentration, mental, ocular and circulatory problems, growth retardation, skin problems such as blemishes and acne, hypoglycemia, premature hair loss, nervousness, anemia and premenstrual syndrome.

Food sources: Brewer's yeast, cereals, liver, kidneys, dairy products, eggs, fish, raisins, cantaloupe, cabbage, carrots, asparagus and green vegetables.

While all of the B vitamins are important, folic acid (B9) and cobalamin, commonly called vitamin B12, are often deficient in people with active celiac disease. Although these two vitamins work hand-in-hand in the creation of healthy blood cells, we will review them separately.

Folic acid (B9)
Functions: Precursor to vitamin B12 absorption, indispensable in the production of nucleic acids (RNA and DNA) and for the division of body cells, necessary for proper brain and nervous system function, increases appetite, stimulates the production of hydrochloric acid in the stomach, prevents anemia, essential during pregnancy for normal fetal development, and increases resistance to disease.

Signs and symptoms of deficiencies: Birth defects in the newborn, anemia, cracks or lesions around the mouth, red and smooth tongue (glossitis), painful mouth and tongue, dull hair, important neurological changes (mental confusion, depression, schizophrenia), fatigue, general weakness, irritability, insomnia and memory loss.

Food sources: Spinach, asparagus, beets, cabbage, chicory, turnip, potatoes, broccoli, lima beans, avocados, dates, prunes, strawberries, liver, kidneys, lamb, cottage cheese, yeast and rice.

Folic acid has many antagonists or enemies that suppress its effect in the body. Many medications (birth control pill, sulfa drugs) and alcohol, as well as cooking heat can destroy this precious vitamin.

Vitamin B12

Functions: Together with folic acid, it is essential to the production of every cell, especially the red blood cell, prevents anemia, necessary for the synthesis of RNA and DNA, supports the nervous, circulatory and female reproductive systems, indispensable for maintaining the myelin sheath around the nerves, and helps to prevent allergies as well as adrenal gland exhaustion.

Signs and symptoms of deficiencies: Chronic fatigue, decrease in mental capacities (concentration, memory), lethargy, loss of interest, menstrual problems, pernicious anemia, asthma, itching, eczema, chest pain, insomnia, vertigo, adrenal exhaustion, loss of balance, numbness and tingling in fingers and toes.

Food sources: Liver, kidneys, beef, lamb, pork, fatty fish, chicken, seafood and eggs.

Certain factors are detrimental to proper vitamin B12 absorption such as the birth control pill, a prolonged iron deficiency, alcohol, stressful situations, sleeping pills, pregnancy and a vegetarian diet. Deficiency is rather rare in babies and young children but it may occur in adolescents.

Vitamin C (ascorbic acid)

Functions: Important in the formation of collagen used in the growth and repair of body tissue cells, gums, blood vessels, bones and teeth, accelerates healing, prevents hemorrhaging, helps the body absorb iron, fights infection, supports the cardiovascular system, protects against cancer by its antioxidant action, aids mental clarity and combats stress.

Signs and symptoms of deficiencies: Pyorrhea (loosening of teeth), allergies, eczema, slipped discs, stiff neck, eye problems, scurvy (bleeding gums), nosebleeds, contusions, hemorrhoids, repeated infections (sore throat, cold, flu) and poor circulation.

Food sources: Green leafy vegetables, alfalfa, asparagus, carrots, celery, tomatoes, watercress, beets, rosehips, citrus fruits, kiwis, berries, chicken liver, rabbit heart and liver, skimmed milk, parsley, peppers and acerola.

The antagonists to vitamin C are stress, fatigue, tobacco use, alcohol consumption, a diet high in nitrates and prolonged cooking time.

Minerals

Certain minerals are also indispensable to the human body. Some of these regulate the water and acid-alkaline balance in the body. They participate in nerve transmission, muscle contraction, cell permeability, blood and bone formation, protein metabolism, energy production and glandular hormonal secretion. A constant and adequate mineral flow insures that cells function normally and maintains good health. Since all elements work in collaboration, a deficiency of one mineral can alter the chain of life, rendering other nutrients useless or inefficient. Although all minerals and trace minerals are essential to good health, we will discuss only a few of which can be deficient in the body if celiac disease goes undiscovered or untreated.

Potassium, sodium and chloride are three minerals that work together and are also called electrolytes. When suffering from persistent diarrhea or vomiting, a person can become dehydrated, and this situation can often lead to an electrolyte imbalance. Severe damage to the duodenum and jejunum can also disturb proper absorption of these vital minerals. Fortunately, blood work can quickly establish an accurate diagnosis and proper fluid and mineral intake can be restored.

Potassium

Functions: Maintains a healthy nervous system and a regular heart rhythm, helps prevent strokes, aids in proper muscle contraction, works with sodium to control the body's water balance, normalizes blood pressure, helps dispose of body waste through the kidneys, and helps in clear thinking by supplying the brain with oxygen.

Signs and symptoms of deficiencies: Acne, constipation, dyspepsia, nausea, diarrhea, physical and mental fatigue, cardiac irregularities, insomnia, dry skin, thirst, hypertension, edema and hypoglycemia.

Food sources: Dairy products, poultry, legumes, tofu, apples, oranges, bananas, raisins, dates, figs, peaches, kiwis, grapefruit, peanuts, unrefined molasses, sunflower seeds, tomatoes, potatoes, squash and seaweeds.

Sodium

Functions: Works in synergy with potassium to regulate heartbeats as well as water and acid-base balance in the body, essential for nerve stimulation, muscle contraction, stomach acid production, oxygen transport and prevents heat prostration or sunstroke.

Signs and symptoms of deficiencies: Indigestion, nausea, flatulence, hypoglycemia, difficulty in digesting carbohydrates, muscular atrophy, cardiac degeneration, weight loss and neuralgic pain.

Food sources: Salt, seafood, carrots, beets, artichokes, dried beef, kidneys, meats, kelp, alfalfa, dandelion, ginger and slippery elm.

Chloride

Functions: Regulates blood alkaline-acid balance, works in synergy with sodium and potassium, aids in cleansing body wastes by helping the liver to function, and is a constituent of hydrochloric acid.

Signs and symptoms of deficiencies: Vomiting, loss of hair and teeth in the case of severe deficiency, psychomotor defects, memory loss and growth retardation.

Food sources: Salt, kelp, olives, vegetables and meats.

Calcium
Functions: Formation of strong bones and teeth, maintains a regular heartbeat and the transmission of nerve impulse, necessary to acid-alkaline balance, facilitates muscle growth and contraction, prevents muscle cramps, essential to blood clotting, regulates blood pressure, and helps to metabolize iron.

Signs and symptoms of deficiencies: Muscle cramps, numbness of limbs, heart palpitations, nervous breakdown, osteoporosis, insomnia, menstrual cramps, brittle nails and teeth decay.

Food sources: Dairy products, sardine and salmon with bones, beef liver, soya, cabbage, dandelion, sesame seeds, nuts, almonds, figs, dates, legumes, broccoli and green leafy vegetables.

Magnesium
Functions: Necessary to maintain acid-alkaline balance, vital to enzyme activity, plays a role in carbohydrate and mineral metabolism (calcium, phosphorus, sodium, potassium and vitamin C) and in RNA and DNA synthesis, acts on nerves and muscles, promotes healthy teeth and bones, supports the nervous system (antistress mineral), regulates blood pressure, prevents cardiovascular problems and calcium deposits (kidney stones and gallstones).

Signs and symptoms of deficiencies: Mental confusion, dizziness, anxiety, heart palpitation, heart disease, high blood pressure, headache, muscle tremors, muscle weakness, twitching, insomnia, irritability, depression, loss of appetite, lethargy, nausea and diarrhea.

Food sources: Fish, seafood, onions, spinach, corn, green vegetables, soya, nuts, almonds, sesame seeds, apples, peaches, figs, lemons, grapefruit, brown rice, whole grains and chlorophyll.

Iron

Functions: Transports oxygen to the red blood cells, necessary to the production of hemoglobin and certain enzymes, increases vitality and immunity, regulates B vitamins metabolism, and prevents fatigue and anemia.

Signs and symptoms of deficiencies: Anemia, shortness of breath, dizziness, constipation, lack of appetite and concentration, pallor, general fatigue, brittle hair, hair loss, and nails that are spoon-shaped or have ridges running lengthwise.

Food sources: Beef liver, red meats, egg yolks, fish, oyster, whole cereals, unrefined molasses, parsley, green leafy vegetables, asparagus, cabbage, beans, beets, nuts, raisins, figs, apricots, avocados, legumes, kelp, nettle and dandelion.

Zinc

Functions: Important for proteins and phosphorus synthesis, aids in the digestion of carbohydrates, helps in the formation of insulin, protects the liver from chemical damage, assists the immune system in fighting infection, accelerates healing time for wounds and burns, promotes night vision, acuity of taste and smell, as well as mental alertness, supports a healthy reproductive system, and protects against prostate problems.

Signs and symptoms of deficiencies: Anorexia, spots on the fingernails, lack of resistance to infection, infertility in men, prostate problems, growth retardation, loss of taste and anemia.

Food sources: Cheese, liver, sprouted seeds and cereals, sunflower seeds, brewer's yeast, mushrooms, spinach, soya beans, oyster, eggs, meats and mustard.

Friendly bacteria

Celiac disease, especially if the disease has been active for a prolonged period of time before diagnosis, has a devastating effect on the intestinal flora. Indeed, intestinal "friendly bacteria" are ravaged and perturbed when faced with an intestinal disease. The intestine shelters millions of bacteria of different species. Non-pathogen bacteria are called "probiotics", which means "for life", a well-deserved name when we consider the numerous health benefits they provide.

Probiotics have an important role to play in food digestion and the subsequent assimilation of vital nutritive elements. They help ensure the proper permeability of the intestinal lining and optimal immune system efficiency. Friendly intestinal bacteria are necessary to the production of B and K vitamins and probably play a role in the prevention of allergies. Furthermore, they have an antibacterial effect and help prevent the growth of undesirable microorganisms, including candida yeast overgrowth and bacteria that cause disease. Probiotics protect us from the many adverse conditions we are subjected to, such as stress, radiation, pollution, and an inadequate diet. A healthy intestinal flora promotes regular intestinal transit and elimination, hence preventing fermentation and excessive putrefaction that cause flatulence.

Certain elements that can inhibit the friendly flora are refined foods, sugar, caffeine, alcoholic beverages, tobacco, antibiotics, steroids, oral contraceptives and vaccination. These factors can cause an imbalance between the different populations of pathogen and non-pathogen bacteria residing in the intestine. While a healthy colon should contain at least 85 percent friendly bacteria and 15 percent coliform bacteria, the typical colon bacteria count is often the reverse. A perturbation of the bacterial equilibrium can be brought on by persistent diarrhea or because of an inadequate diet (by lack of absorption of nutritional elements) as it is frequently the case with celiacs.

To restore the situation and repopulate the intestinal flora, a supplement of "friendly bacteria" is advisable. The most common strains of probiotics are *Lactobacillus acidophilus* and *Bifidobacterium bifidum*, though others can complete the formula. Certain brands use lactose, so if you are lactose intolerant, it is important to verify all ingredients closely. These supplements need to be kept in the refrigerator.

Digestive enzymes

Every normal function of every single cell in our body relies on enzymes. Made out of protein, the thousands of known enzymes play a role in virtually all body activities. Without going through a biochemical transformation themselves, enzymes function as catalysts for thousands of specific biochemical reactions, from digestion to the repair of damaged tissue. In other words, enzymes allow the transformation of a substance into another, as the body needs it.

As each enzyme has a specialized function, digestive enzymes convert food particles into usable nutrients for our body. Enzymes are present in raw, natural foods. Raw foods contain the very enzymes needed to insure their own digestion. Cooking and processing deplete foods of enzymes. The longer food is cooked, the fewer enzymes are left. All people with less than perfect health should opt for a digestive enzyme supplement to promote optimal assimilation of their food. Since celiac disease can severely hinder food absorption, a nutritional aid such as digestive enzymes is worth investigating.

Although it is difficult for the naked eye to detect a nutritional deficiency, some symptoms of enzymatic insufficiency are flagrant. They include drowsiness following a meal, a bloating sensation spreading even way up under the ribcage, abdominal distention, burping, flatulence, a feeling of "being still full" when the next meal comes around, and even persistent fatigue. These symptoms can also indicate a lack of hydrochloric acid, which is found in many digestive enzyme formulas.

Digestive enzymes each have their particular function. Lipase breaks down fats, while protease takes care of proteins, and amylase and maltase ensure carbohydrate digestion. Lactase breaks down lactose in dairy products. Enzyme formulas abound on the market. Two types are well known; plant enzymes, which usually include papain and bromelain, and pancreatic enzymes, which contain pancreatin that is derived from animal pancreas. Take enzymes before meals to aid digestion or between meals to reduce pain and inflammation. The choice of a plant or pancreatic enzyme depends on personal requirements (with or without hydrochloric acid) and preference. People suffering from an ulcer or taking certain medications should avoid hydrochloric acid.

Phytotherapy

Phytotherapy is the use of herbs and other plants to promote health. For the celiac population, herbal medicine is very helpful when it comes to relieving troublesome symptoms rather than for treating the disease itself. Although the plant kingdom offers a world of possibilities, we will discuss only a few plants, aiming mostly at those able to provide relief of the digestive and intestinal discomfort that so often accompanies celiac disease.

Slippery elm has always been known for its soothing quality; its inner bark has important medicinal value. It is an official drug of the *United States Pharmacopoeia*. Highly nutritious, it would be an excellent herb to have at hand in case of famine. It is a mucilaginous herb, which means it expands when mixed with water; this feature facilitates soothing and healing of the stomach and intestinal mucous membranes. Slippery elm is much recommended in case of diarrhea; it normalises bowel movements, soothes all inflamed tissues (stomach, bowels, kidneys), and helps heal ulcers and the entire intestinal tract. It is also helpful in the treatment of colitis, hemorrhoids, digestive problems, diverticulitis and even sore throats.

Marshmallow, which is diuretic and emollient, benefits the urinary, intestinal and respiratory systems. Like slippery elm, it is mucilaginous, so it coats, soothes and heals all inflamed mucous membranes. It is used for bladder problems, emphysema, kidney stones, to increase lactation, and to relieve inflammation caused by gastritis or diarrhea.

Aloes Vera is one of the most popular and well-known plants. It is a great healer that has been used for centuries. It seems to contain a pain relieving agent and starts to heal on contact. It prevents and draws out infection while promoting quick healing of wounds by removing the dead skin and stimulating the normal growth of living cells. It is a very versatile herb that can offer relief from allergies, burns, digestive discomfort, ulcers, colitis, herpes and insect stings.

Lobelia is considered one of the most potent single herbs; its antispasmodic action makes it quite remarkable. As it relieves spasms, it can be very effective to diminish intestinal cramping, while having a relaxant effect on the individual. It is useful as an analgesic for pain, for allergies, asthma, bronchitis, headache, insomnia and nervous tension. It is a versatile herb that adapts to the situation; its adaptability makes it an excellent product to keep at hand, but out of reach of children.

The name **alfalfa** means "Father of all foods". It has also been called the "King of plants" because it is extremely rich in vitamins and minerals and is often considered to be a tonic herb. Alfalfa contains iron, calcium, magnesium, phosphorus, sulfur, chlorine, sodium, potassium, silicon and trace elements, while being a good source of beta-carotene and vitamin K. It provides all eight of the essential amino acids and the highest chlorophyll content of any plant. Its high nutritive value explains why it is used as a base in many tonics and vitamin formulas. It helps fight allergies, bursitis and loss of appetite, increases lactation, facilitates digestion and soothes intestinal troubles. For certain sensitive people that cannot tolerate vitamin supplements, alfalfa can provide a healthy gluten-free alternative.

Many plant combinations are available on the market; grouping of herbs and plants offers complementary synergic effects. Others plants worth mentioning for their soothing and healing properties on the digestive and intestinal systems are fennel, catnip, chamomile, ginger, papaya, psyllium, peppermint and Taheebo tea also called pau d'arco.

134

CHAPTER EIGHT

The psychological aspect of the disease

Optimal health is the balance between the different dimensions of our lives. Healthy living incorporates all aspects of a person's life, including physical, mental, emotional and spiritual. It was in 1943 that Abraham Maslow, a member of the Chicago dynasty of psychologists and sociologists, published his theory of human motivation. Since 1954, this theory on the hierarchy of needs is used to better understand fundamental requirements in all domains.

The easiest way to comprehend the hierarchy of needs is to watch a newborn. His first needs are physiological; he demands food and warmth. As he grows older, his needs will increase; he will then pursue safety and love. Further ahead, as a toddler, he will crave social interaction, until as an adolescent or young adult, he will search for ways to fulfill his need for self-esteem or self-worth and recognition of others. At this moment, he will begin to trust himself and feel that he can influence others. It will then be time for self-actualization, a time to follow his calling, meaning the possibility to become anything he wants to be (a musician, a writer...). The dominant need is always shifting. For example, if we observe a musician lost in the self-actualization of playing music, when he eventually realises that he is hungry; this primary or physiological need then becomes the most pressing one to satisfy. We have to realise that the term "satisfaction" is relative to the present moment.

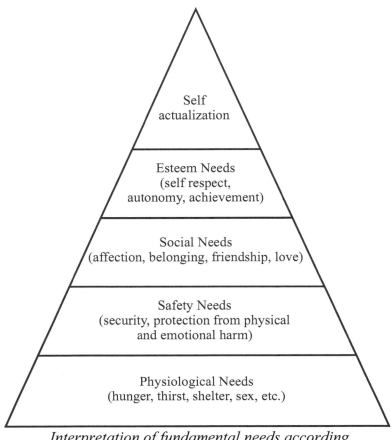

Interpretation of fundamental needs according
to Abraham Maslow

The basic needs of a person burdened by an illness are not necessarily the same as for one that is healthy and energetic. However, the course of celiac disease differs for each individual, and is even in constant change for a same person, so the hierarchy of needs will change according to good and bad days.

Initially, we have to fulfill physiological needs that support life such as hunger, thirst, shelter and clothing. For as long as these are not satisfied, all of the person's energy will be concentrated at this level. For celiacs, food is often a major challenge; learning what is acceptable to a gluten-free diet, where to buy such food, and even how to prepare it will necessitate some get-up-and-go. This step can be conquered with a display of good will and effort.

The second echelon of needs to assume is that of security, including protection from physical and emotional harm, an income to see to our comfort and a pleasant home. This step can cause some concerns depending on the individual's state of health. Some celiacs can go on with a normal life routine while others are suffering to the point of having to abandon their jobs on a temporary, or unfortunately, sometimes permanent basis. The monetary shortage that often follows can have harsh consequences, such as having to let go of a home that has now become too expensive, which in turn leads to a difficult emotional state due to such unsettling stress. This sad and exaggerated picture aims at a better comprehension of the possible influence of celiac disease on one's life. It is often difficult to understand what nightmarish modifications a disease can bring to one's existence, especially when the treatment is as simple as a diet. Unfortunately, unless the celiac diagnosis is made quickly, health complications are real and can lead to dramatic lifestyle changes.

The third hierarchic level is filled by social needs such as affection and a sense of belonging, including friendship and love. Although for many celiacs, this does not cause a problem, the real impact is proportional to the severity of the disease, to the broadmindedness of people around, and even to one's own acceptance of the condition. Many celiacs continue to enjoy outings to the restaurant with friends and participate in family gatherings while respecting their gluten-free diet. Regrettably, some admit to having gradually cut all exterior links as they found it too difficult to integrate their special dietary needs to a social life. Some celiacs sadly confide that even close relatives find it too complicated to invite them to share family meals.

As you are undoubtedly starting to understand, it is difficult to climb the ladder of fundamental needs towards self-esteem (fourth level) when the preceding ones are more or less satisfied. Most people feel the need to be esteemed based on a solid reality or achievement; they want to be recognized and respected by others. This satisfaction leads to a feeling of self-confidence, self-respect, prestige and self-control. It is rather contradictory to think of exerting a certain influence in our midst when one can hardly control his state of health.

According to Maslow, self-realization was defined by a phrase that went something like this: "What a man can be, he must become." When all of our most important needs are fulfilled, it is then time to choose our occupations according to personal preferences. Whether it is music, traveling or writing, self-actualization is the goal to aim for. Though the way there may seem longer to a celiac, busy learning about the disease and how to live with its implications, this does not in any way exclude the possibility to reach the ultimate objective.

It is known that when a life-changing event takes place, one will often have to deal with a grief process. When a person is diagnosed with a lifetime disease, whether it is easy to control or not, the news is still shocking. Each person experiences grief differently, dealing with feelings as they come. The feeling of bereavement is similar when it is your child or a loved-one that is diagnosed with celiac disease.

At first, denial about having the disease and the all-encompassing changes that accompany it is common. During the denial phase, newly diagnosed celiacs will often refuse to adhere to a gluten-free diet, as the consequences of the condition are still not clear. Outbursts such as, "I'm already sick, what is one more slice of pizza going to change?" are vehemently thrown about.

As the reality of the situation gradually sets in, anger and depression enter the picture. Thoughts such as, "Why did this happen to me?" run through a person's mind. At this point, the individual becomes conscious of all the changes celiac disease will bring into his life. The idea of eating out at someone else's home or at the restaurant and having to explain the special diet will trigger anxiety.

Finally, there is acceptation that as far as disease goes, this one is not so bad. Phrases such as, "At least this disease doesn't have any medication, needles or hospitalization, just a diet to follow!" describe this new phase. At this point, the realization that excluding gluten will also eliminate the nasty symptoms is often incentive enough to accept this new situation.

Some people will need moral support to get through the emotions of the grief process. Share your worries and frustrations with close relatives, your doctor or a psychologist. You can also join a celiac support group where you will have the possibility to communicate with people that have or are crossing the same path as you. Allow celiac disease to become a starting point towards good health and happiness.

CHAPTER NINE

Testimonials

The following testimonials are authentic and sincere. The goal is not to have people feel sorry for the ill-fated celiacs. To the contrary, the objective sought after is that these few pages will help people recognise the symptoms of the disease and its true consequences on a person's life; this would bring much needed comprehension and perhaps, hope for an easier life for the celiac individual. These testimonials also want to demonstrate that after months or even years of suffering, once the diagnosis is finally established, life as it should be can return, letting people go on to a happy and gratifying existence. I am deeply grateful to the people who accepted to share their personal stories with us.

Corentin

It was in November 2001 that we discovered that our four years old son suffers from celiac disease. Corentin's first symptoms appeared soon after birth; he would vomit within ten minutes of each bottle feeding. He was a very small baby that was born five weeks premature. His pediatrician thought he did not tolerate that specific brand of milk, so we tried others. He was fed only milk until he was one year old, so I did not introduce cereals until then.

It was when we tried to add more foods to his diet that his weight started to drop; he refused all dairy products, and each time he ate cheese, yogurt or cake (containing milk but also gluten), he would have diarrhea. Thinking he was allergic to milk, we eliminated all milk products. This went on for three years before he was finally tested for allergies, including dairy products. The results were negative. Diarrhea and vomiting persisted for another year.

In November 2001, he contracted a very persistent bout of gastroenteritis. The doctor decided to test him for gluten intolerance when he noticed the continuous weight loss. I must add that the doctor did not think of testing for celiac disease earlier, even with his frequent bouts of gastroenteritis. What a shame! Blood screening results were not all positive, only antigliadin antibodies showed up at 138 units while the normal level is 45. He then underwent a small bowel biopsy. The results came back negative, but the doctor wanted to repeat the biopsy for confirmation, as it would seem that the sample was taken from the wrong part of the small bowel.

Since January 2002, Corentin has been following a gluten-free diet and his state of health has improved though without any remarkable weight gain. He accepts his condition without too much complaining, but he is still frail. Lately, he contracted another bout of gastroenteritis; he was vomiting again and complaining of stomach pain. It is not always easy to manage all this. His character can be difficult; he is very possessive, as he does not have a lot of contact with kids his own age. The doctor wants him to avoid daycare as an extra precaution.

The pediatrician wants me to reintroduce gluten foods in a year's time, but I don't think I will do so. Each time he deviates from the gluten-free diet, he pays the price. His weight is still four kilograms under what is normal for his age.

For us parents, it is not easy; we must always be watchful of what he eats. We have to say "no" when he sees a chocolate cake. We are careful not to tempt him with foods. It is difficult! As long as he is doing well, we are in good spirits, but as soon as he complains of a stomachache, we remember that he really suffers from a disease. Our relatives believe that since he only has to follow a diet, it is a disease of little importance, that it could have been worse. Since they are not confronted with it each day, it is easy for them to say. The diet is constraining as nothing must tempt him, not even a piece of bread! We buy his food in a specialty store. Only his health matters!

Sylvie, Corentin's mother

Henri Roger

As soon as I was born, I found myself at La Crèche d'Youville orphanage, going back and forth from the Ste-Justine hospital and the orphanage. At first, the doctor diagnosed a dolicho mega sigmoid (means long) and megacolon. He gave me a severe diet to follow, but it did not help. At six and a half years old, a foster home took me in, but sadly, I was too weak to run, jump and play like normal kids did. I was allergic to milk and everything I ate went right through me. I suffered a considerable growth delay.

When I was between the ages of six and twelve years old, my adoptive mother was discouraged; she got up at night to give me some medication against diarrhea and stomachaches, but still, I was up all night running to the bathroom. The next day, I would go back to school, but sometimes I was so sick that I just had to stay home. I was terribly weak; because of this, I had to repeat grade two. At the age of six, I measured 84 centimeters (33 inches) in height and weight 15 kilograms (33 pounds). Yes, you read right! Even the doctor was amazed. He was then treating me for milk intolerance and for the nervous system. I had a lot of difficulty walking; my mother had to carry me up the stairs. When I watched other kids my age walk and run, I knew something was wrong with me. The adults around us, and even some close relatives used to say to my mother who was a certified nurse: "Why did you choose that child as a foster child? You should have left him where he was, that child will never amount to much!" A schoolteacher even called me "retarded"; I felt humiliated and degraded in front of all these people who did not understand me. I suffered from a feeling of inferiority and a lack of self-confidence. I was scared of everything; I was unable to move ahead during my childhood years. I owe my life and my health to my mother, who despite all of these people, adopted me at age twelve. Although the disease was not yet diagnosed, her constant presence, patience and affection soothed a lot of my physical and psychological pain.

I was often absent during my first year of high school. I was fourteen years old and always sick with diarrhea, vomiting, headaches, pain in my legs and general weakness. I even had a broken arm at that time. I worked as a packer on the weekends. I finally finished high school. At age nineteen, I enrolled in the National Defense for a three-year term while pursuing my studies. For four years, I seemed to be in remission; I was fairly well with just an occasional bout of diarrhea and weakness. While on assignment in another country, this darned disease caught up with me again. I came back to Canada for treatment, but it was useless. In the following years, I continued to work and study while being haunted by this unnamed disease. At work one day, I was lifting a box that weighted about 11 kilograms (25 pounds - a weight easily lifted by a twelve year old child) and I dropped it. That's when I realized that my health was deteriorating rapidly, especially since I only weighted 43 kilograms (95 pounds) at the time. After this incident, I asked for time off to consult a gastroenterologist.

This doctor examined me and asked a few questions concerning my symptoms, behavior and general state of health. He decided to hospitalize me for a week and have me undergo routine exams. Following many tests, including blood screening, gastroscopy, endoscopy and rectoscopy, he diagnosed me with severe gluten enteropathy. Convinced that I had generalized cancer, relief gave me the impression of two tons being lifted from my shoulders. A dietician came to visit and told me I simply had to follow a diet for the rest of my life and she wished me good luck.

With time, I discovered that I react very strongly to air-borne flour. Even the smell of pastries or restaurant cooking fumes bothers me to the point of setting off all my symptoms. In no time, I become aggressive, along with a headache, anxiety and stomachache; even my visual acuity diminishes. I sometimes react so strongly that I must ask for help to drive my car back home. Humiliation and discouragement are also part of this disease.

Shortly before I was diagnosed, when I was about thirty-two years old, I had a very upsetting experience. I was tired of this famous disease. One day, my aunt who worked as a nurse at the time, referred me to a general practitioner while mentioning that I was nervous, anxious and aggressive. This doctor gave me a prescription for Valium, and added something called opium camphor tannin to hopefully relieve the everlasting diarrhea. I took this medication for a year. Let me tell you I was calm, to the point of being indolent. At this time, I was working for the government and I was less than efficient. My employer realized something was wrong with me; I was not working at my best and I didn't care. My superior gave me a week off to get that medication out of my system. It should be noted that this medication had no effect whatsoever on the disease. Getting rid of the side effects of that medication was very difficult. Only my mother lent me a helping hand as I was unpleasant, bitter with life, discouraged and was even thinking of suicide. I prayed for help facing this disease, and also for a woman who would accept me as I was. At age thirty-six, I got married, and I was finally diagnosed at age thirty-eight.

In short, I was diagnosed with a severe case of celiac disease, and then, in 1999, they added osteopenia (diminution of bone density) of the vertebral column with high risk for fracture, accompanied by reflux esophagitis.

Testimonial from Linda, Roger's wife:
I first met Roger in 1983; he was skinny, short and had black hair. From the start, he told me: "I want to tell you something. I'm sick, I don't know what I have and the doctors can't find out. I eat but don't keep anything in. Now that I've told you everything, it's up to you to decide if you want to see me again." After six months, we were married. To top off his other symptoms, he also had swollen feet; he was exhausted and said he had white stools. The doctor gave him B12 vitamins. He ate normally, but still lost weight. I was astounded by how much food such a small man could gobble up.

At the beginning of 1985, Roger had become aggressive and he knew he was not doing well at all. That was when he was finally diagnosed. He followed the diet and there was a lot of improvement, but the diarrhea persisted as well as the fatigue. We then joined up with the Celiac disease Foundation. Their list of foods to avoid was even longer. To tell the truth, I had a hard time accepting it; everything had become so complicated. A simple diet was turning into a nightmare. I'm not sure how long it took me to realized and truly understand how serious the situation was. To cook without gluten was hell. After eighteen years, I still have a hard time making a good cake, though I can make bread that he likes. If Roger consumes gluten by mistake, he becomes very tense, nothing can please him, and then, the usual symptoms appear. Still, we have a very normal life. Today, he's in almost normal health and sometimes more energetic than I am.

Roger continues…

There were some good moments, but the disease always resurfaced. I was unable to eat like everyone else or to do things like everyone else, and I suffered from a significant growth delay. I apologize for the expression but "sick as a dog" summarizes it well. At the present time, I'm not very tall or very big, but I'm here. I'm married to a wonderful woman who was able to understand me and to help me follow the strict diet. It was more difficult for my relatives; I was even rejected by some. They just found my diet too complicated to follow. Since I wasn't able to go to the restaurant or out for a beer, I lost all my friends. When I'm invited to a gathering, I bring along my gluten-free food, but everybody does not appreciate this kind of thing. However, it is my health we are talking about.

As I write this, I'm fifty-five years old and at 1.65 meters (5 feet 4 inches), I weight between 56 and 63 kilograms (125 and 140 pounds) depending on the season. I live with a severe case of celiac disease so I don't take it lightly. Cheating could be disastrous to my health. I still suffer from long-term complications such as gastric reflux that can lead to esophagitis, and advanced osteopenia, which to date, does not seem to improve even with medication. So I continue my gluten-free diet and take the medication proposed by the gastroenterologist. For the last five years, symptoms have been less severe. I know research on celiac disease is continuing. Although for now, I'm in control of the disease, I would like to eat like everyone else someday. I still have hope that good results will come out of all the research.

Henri Roger

Emily

For as long as I can remember, every time I ate porridge or barley, I immediately felt sick. As a kid of five or six years old, I didn't know much about allergies and neither did my parents. This pattern went on for years and I always felt sick.

Later on, when I mentioned this to the doctor, adding that I always felt tired and anxious, his answer was that I was surely a bit depressed and he handed me a prescription for antidepressants. The first time was when I was eighteen years old. I was given a month off because he thought work was the reason I was stressed and the cause of my depression. Those pills helped me feel a bit better, but shortly after, I started feeling run-down and depressed again. I can't remember exactly how many times I was given antidepressants, but certainly seven or eight times.

At one point, the headaches and the intestinal problems started. I had to make sure to stay close to a bathroom. I can't remember exactly when the headaches began, but I was twenty-seven years old during my last pregnancy and I had mentioned them to my doctor then. He had answered that I would be fine after the baby was born. Strangely, while I was pregnant was the time I felt the best. In 1984, I underwent an EEG (electroencephalogram) and a brain scan, though I was certain my problem didn't stem from there.

I wondered if it could have been an allergy, but the doctor did not react to the suggestion. Another doctor finally referred me to an allergist. The tests showed an allergy to chicken! Chicken! So I avoided chicken for a long time, but still the headaches and diarrhea persisted.

All this time, I felt worse and worse; I thought life wasn't worth living and that it would have been a good thing if I could just die (thinking about dying seemed normal to me then).

I started to read books about health, going through everything I could find. I found a few diseases that described how I felt. Crohn's disease? Celiac disease? Concerning celiac disease, my doctor told me: "Oh no! You're much too fat for that. I have celiac patients and they are all thin." I was so depressed and tired of feeling sick; I just didn't know where to turn next. I also had itchy red blotches that lasted a very long time. This was in 1991 or 1992. It was much later that I learned from the Celiac Association that if one is intolerant to wheat and has a rash, there is a good chance of having celiac disease.

As I thought I might be suffering from wheat intolerance, I stopped eating bread, and I watched out for wheat, but I didn't know there was wheat in everything we eat… even in ice cream. I didn't know yet that I was intolerant to dairy products.

Two different doctors finally tested me for celiac disease, a couple of times in fact. I told them I wasn't eating wheat for two years so the result would be negative. One doctor answered that if I had celiac disease, he would find it. According to the Celiac Association, this is not the case. Of course, the tests were negative.

During the year 1992, I had a barium enema and two colonoscopies. I underwent these tests because I had a lot of mucus in my stools, and I insisted that it was not normal. They found two benign polyps but I still had no explanation for the mucus. The doctor (in Ontario at that time) wanted to see me every six to twelve weeks and at one point, he told me I needed a psychiatrist. I had two more colonoscopies later after I moved. Now, the doctor wants to do a colonoscopy every six months, but I decided I didn't need the aggravation.

At age sixty-three, we moved to New Brunswick. I saw the sign in front of Gisèle's house and decided to give natural medicine a try. What did

I have to lose? Well, less then a week after my visit to her clinic, I already felt a lot better. She suggested the possibility of an intolerance to wheat and to other gluten-containing grains, dairy products and corn.

What a change in my life! I can now wake up without a headache in the morning and be happy I'm alive. No more depression. I still feel pain in my joints when I sit for too long a period of time without moving, perhaps arthritis. The painful joints are far from recent; I remember that in the early 80's, I already had a hard time going down the stairs in the morning.

I joined the Celiac Association two years ago, and they help me with nutritional advice. I treat myself as if I had celiac disease even though I'll never be officially diagnosed as such. As long as I avoid gluten, I feel fine. When I think of my life quality now, what a difference… I wish I had met Gisèle earlier…. Thank you Gisèle.

Emily Phillips

Simon

My name is Julie. My son Simon is five years old, and he's autistic as is my brother Sébastien who is twenty-four years old. Simon was my first child; I was twenty-four years old then. My pregnancy was problem-free although the delivery had to be provoked and lasted twelve hours. I still remember very well the first time I saw my son; he didn't cry, he was on my stomach and seemed to be looking at me with his little eyes. He acted like a normal baby; he enjoyed breastfeeding, he cried normally, he smiled, he liked to be cuddled and had lively eyes.

His development proceeded normally until he had his fifteen months immunization (MRM). It was then that he started to scream at night; he would yell every time he needed something. Before this vaccination, I had noticed that he would clap his hands when he was happy, and that his speech was almost non-existent, but the vaccination seemed to have triggered off the worst. After a few months of denial, I decided to proceed with the investigation to establish a diagnosis. He suffers from a "pervasive developmental disorder" or PDD, in the spectrum of autism, what we could call a light case of autism. The very next day, I began my search for a solution. My mother gave me a pile of magazines published by different autistic associations. They mentioned Lovaas; so I contacted a psychologist specialized in applied behavior analysis (ABA), a method for teaching autistics.

My research continued. I also discovered that some symptoms of autism have biological causes such as intestinal troubles, *Candida albicans* and food intolerances. Vitamin therapy was cited as helping at different levels. A gluten-free and casein-free diet was also mentioned. I went on to discover that gluten is a wheat component as well as that of other grain cereals. I remember thinking that there was wheat everywhere. I was ready to try anything, so I bought gluten-free products, as well as soya milk to replace cow's milk. I also stocked up on vitamin B6 and vitamin C, magnesium, folic acid, and dimethyglycine (DMG). Sugar was also eliminated from Simon's diet.

After only a few days of taking the supplements, Simon, who was usually angry, became happy, more sociable; he even waved "bye-bye" to people in an adequate fashion and he was also more alert and present to his environment. I was certain that Simon also had an intestinal problem and perhaps candida. He had very soft stools, too soft, not diarrhea but close, and probably stomachaches and headaches too. I contacted a naturopath. Simon definitely suffered from candida and his intestines were permeable. Normally, healthy intestines are impermeable; they do not let any molecule of food filter through. Contrarily, when they are permeable, they let intruders sift through and these find their way into the blood. These molecules are invaders in the body as well as in the brain and they act as a drug, or rather the brain perceives them as such. This explains why autistic persons have some strange behaviors. Simon has been seeing a naturopath for a year and a half and has been following his gluten-free diet for two years. He has also received several treatments including one to clear out heavy metals and his intestines are now as good as new. Still today, if Simon strays from his diet, gluten and casein alike, he seems drugged and is not at all present. He becomes angry, he does not sleep as well at night and his stools are softer.

I consider that the gluten-free diet has greatly contributed to his progress and that he wouldn't have achieved so much without it. Simon is now a joyous and easy to live with child. He sleeps well in contrast to the terrible night terrors I had to deal with every night. When his intestinal problems diminished, his sleep improved. He now listens well, and he is attentive to what is going on around him. It is very pleasant to watch him play with his three year old sister, and to hear them laugh together.

He responds well to the ABA therapy and is very computer oriented. Although he still doesn't talk much, the PEP-R (a test to measure the level of development in autistics) confirmed that his development delay is slight compared to his age group. He also underwent an intellectual quotient test, which showed him to be in the low average, so there is no intellectual deficiency. As I report all of these encouraging signs of progress, I am in fact sharing all the comments I get from the different people that work with him. They are all working hard on his language skills. The majority pretends that if Simon could learn to express himself verbally, his autism would scarcely be present, and that he would have all the possibilities of a normal little boy or just about.

Julie Gélinas, Simon's mother

Gisèle

My first memory of abnormal symptoms goes back to when I was fourteen years old. At the time, I suffered from diarrhea much more often than most people. Now that I know that celiac disease usually has a trigger factor, I can link the beginning of my symptoms with the death of a relative.

After many painful and exhausting diarrheic sessions, and a few medical consultations, I excluded dairy products from my diet. Many years went by this way; I constantly dragged along intestinal problems, digestive discomfort, often in the form of heartburn or bloating, as well as fatigue. In spite of this, I completed my studies, became a certified nurse, took the time to get married and even had two children. The reintroduction of milk products in my diet during my first pregnancy was short-lived. To insure a good calcium intake, I chose to drink a fortified soya milk formula, which I tolerated better. Though still an unexplained phenomena, the intestinal symptoms were hardly present during the two pregnancies, without any change to my diet, and they returned both times shortly after having the baby.

To avoid the diarrhea "crisis", I began to eliminate certain foods from my diet, starting with spices, acidic foods such as tomatoes and oranges, fibrous vegetables such as broccoli, lettuce and cabbage, as well as barley. Without being aware of it, these restrictions caused me to eat more bread and pasta, since I had a great appetite.

Around the age of twenty-six, after a particularly virulent period of diarrhea and a weight loss of 11 kilograms (25 pounds), I was referred to a well-known gastroenterologist. He admitted me to the hospital for ten days to undergo many medical tests, which were often uncomfortable not to say painful. His goal was to eliminate possibilities of cancer, colitis and celiac sprue disease. I returned home a few pounds lighter, weakened by all the testing, with a frustrating diagnosis of irritable bowel syndrome aggravated by stress. Relieved not to have a terrible disease, I wondered what stress it could be, except for that of having frequent, long and exhausting bouts of diarrhea. I had a calm life, easy children, I worked part-time by choice; a lifestyle some of my friends actually envied. Once I returned home, I went back to the same diet, rich in bread and pasta, which were the foods I craved.

A few years later, around the age of thirty, during a more active and stressful period of my life, including moving, taking on more hours at work, numerous outside activities and the animated lifestyle of a mother of young children, my state of health deteriorated. The diarrhea appeared almost daily, an overwhelming fatigue grabbed a hold of me, and at the same time, I suffered more and more food reactions, all this accompanied with nervousness and anxiety. Having lost faith in allopathic medicine, I directed myself toward a more natural approach.

The naturopath I met was also a medical doctor. Armed with a list of suggested vitamins and minerals and an elimination diet, I was ready to start fighting again. The vegetarian elimination diet consisted of brown rice accompanied with one kind of vegetable a day, with the addition of one new vegetable every fourth day, so I could identify allergenic foods. The diarrhea diminished but did not disappear completely, and I was so weak that I had to take a leave of absence from work once again. Everything that was not absolutely necessary to my children's well-being was scratched off my list of activities. I felt a bit better, but I didn't feel I was progressing. Around this time, I started to suffer from pneumonia each winter, and as I didn't tolerate antibiotics very well, the recovery period was long.

I was visiting a health food store one day when the owner recommended a naturopath. I called this person and following her advice I immediately eliminated wheat, sugar, dairy products (already done) and yeast from my diet. Within three weeks, the diarrhea had disappeared and the fatigue seemed less constraining. There was hope after all. After three months on this diet, I went back to my nursing career, and started courses in naturopathy, which I pursued for many years. Shortly after, I opened a natural health clinic. I was then taking many natural supplements to improve the health of my digestive and intestinal tracts and to boost my weakened immune system. After a year and a half of sticking closely to the diet and supplement program, I was hardly the same person. I worked two jobs, as my clinic was an immediate success, I traveled frequently to keep up with my studies, I studied every free moment I had and I found time to walk every day. My weight went back up to 61 kilograms (135 pounds), an ideal weight for my height. I considered myself intolerant to the above-mentioned foods. Life was fabulous!

Then I discovered spelt flour. I was conscious that spelt contained gluten but secure in the thought that I did not have celiac disease (after all, the doctor had confirmed this), I included spelt into my diet. Wonderful, I tolerated it well! I made myself delicious hot biscuits for breakfast.

Everything was fine. The following year, I discovered sourdough spelt bread and spelt pasta, which increased my daily intake of gluten-containing flour by quite a bit.

I started feeling tired and suffered from occasional diarrhea but without the painful cramps like before. As my numerous interests demanded a lot of energy, I decided to quit my nursing job and to give up a few activities such as hosting conferences and taking part in health fairs.

Many things were happening at the same time; my father was diagnosed with cancer, my girls were now teenagers, the trips out of town for my studies continued, and the overwhelming fatigue was now becoming constant, with a gradually increasing feeling of anxiety and depression. A divorce and a few additional events were enough to force me to take a break from work and to confine myself to bed for many months. The depression became major, the anxiety constant, the pain in my back and muscles was unbearable, and diarrhea came and went, but worse, a feeling of complete exhaustion so intense that just the idea of getting out of bed tired me out. And that is how three years of hell began. I quickly realized that spelt was worsening my condition, so it was eliminated right away but with little relief. The damage was done. With hindsight, I remember that some signs of nutrient malabsorption had been noticeable for a while; my bone were cracking again when I moved, I had fat and mucus in my stools, white spots on my fingernails, a bit of acne, etc.

Looking back, I can trace the exact road I followed. The introduction of spelt in my diet and an occasional food indulgence (after all, I felt good so why not treat myself once in a while) surely led to the unbelievable degradation of my state of health. With worrisome diagnoses such as fibromyalgia, depression and anxiety, my life became a nightmare. The feeling of deep anxiety was omnipresent, while weird symptoms appeared each day such as dizziness, insomnia while I was so tired I didn't know what to do with myself, itching over the whole body, painful hands, and let's not forget muscle weakness and constant back pain. As if that wasn't enough, I became even more intolerant to foods and nutritional supplements, the same ones that had saved me the first time, and to top it off, all strong odors would affect me. From a strong active optimist woman who enjoyed life, I became an anxious and weaken shadow of the woman I used to be, but still very determined to get better. I categorically refused to become another statistic.

I shared my story with you to emphasize the importance of an early diagnosis of celiac disease. After a knowledgeable gastroenterologist assured me that I did not have celiac disease, I chose not to pursue it any further despite my nursing background. That was my biggest mistake. Even without a formal diagnosis of celiac disease, I am now convinced that I suffer from it. Any accidental straying from the gluten-free diet is immediately followed by unmistakable symptoms.

More than two years have gone by, and I am now writing this book and this testimonial. Having left my hometown to follow my heart, and after two years of resting, everything has become quite clear. Since all gluten has been excluded from my diet, life has been a lot easier. Little by little, everything will continue to return to normal and I believe that the best is yet to come.

Gisèle Frenette

Conclusion

Undoubtedly, there is an imperative need for a more efficient way to detect celiac disease. In the meantime, to avoid the amalgam of physical, mental and emotional problems it brings forth, promoting celiac education is still the best tactic. The medical population (doctor, dietician, pharmacist), relatives, friends and all people encountered in our daily routine have to acknowledge celiac disease as an important autoimmune disease with significant sequels, and this even if its treatment seems easy and risk free. Celiac disease research is still seeking the ultimate cure or at least, a way to able celiacs to tolerate gluten-containing foods. A new discovery early in the year 2000 brought hope.

Researchers at the University of Maryland School of Medicine have found that the human protein "zonulin", which regulates the permeability of the intestine, is at increased levels during the acute phase of celiac disease. This discovery suggests that increased levels of zonulin are a contributing factor to the development of celiac disease and other autoimmune disorders such as insulin dependent diabetes, multiple sclerosis and rheumatoid arthritis.

In the *Lancet* medical journal, a doctor named Alessio Fasano explains that zonulin works like a traffic conductor or the gatekeeper of our body's tissues. Our largest gateway is the intestine with its billions of cells. Zonulin opens the spaces between cells allowing some substances to pass through while keeping harmful bacteria and toxins out. He adds: "With celiac disease, we could never understand how a big protein like gluten was getting through to the immune system. People with celiac have an increased level of zonulin, which opens the junctions between the cells. In essence, the gateways are stuck open, allowing gluten and other allergens to pass. Once these allergens get into the immune system, they are attacked by the antibodies." Dr. Fasano believes that zonulin plays a critical role in the modulation of our immune system. For some reason, the zonulin levels go out of whack, and that leads to autoimmune disease. The researchers believe that the increased intestinal permeability is associated with increased levels of zonulin. Dr. Fasano says they are at the threshold of exciting discoveries in this field.[1]

Another interesting discovery came to us from Dr. Luis Sorell and his colleagues from the *Center for Genetic Engineering and Biotechnology* in Havana, Cuba. They are experimenting with a new anti-transglutaminase antibody test, which can accurately diagnose people with celiac disease in less than ten minutes. To determine its accuracy, they evaluate 50 patients with untreated celiac disease along with 40 patients who had other gastrointestinal disorders. The results showed that the experiment was 100% accurate; all of the patients with diagnosed celiac disease tested positive, and all of the patients with other disorders tested negative. Ultimately, this simple test that consist of a nitrocellulose strip like the one used to verify blood sugar levels, could allow the general population to be tested for celiac disease at little cost.

In the last few years, research on all aspects of celiac disease has been emphasized. Each breakthrough brings new hope for a permanent solution in the near future. We must consider ourselves fortunate that celiac disease can be treated without daily medication, painful treatment or surgical procedure. We must always remember to appreciate life and to welcome each good moment with a smile.

Glossary

Acid-alkaline balance: The normal equilibrium between acids and alkalis in the body. The pH (potential of hydrogen) is a measure of the acidity or alkalinity of a solution. It is measured by a scale of zero to fourteen; the lower the pH the more acidic the solution, the higher the pH the more alkaline (or base) the solution. A pH of 7 is neutral. Blood pH has to maintain itself between 7,35 and 7,45. In the body, the body's fluids and electrolytes regulate pH balance. A diet rich in protein is acidifying, while fruits and vegetables are alkalinizing.

Antibody: A substance made by the immune system that recognizes and combines with foreign materials (antigens) that have gotten into the body. Antibodies are one part of the body's natural defense against invasion by germs and other potentially harmful substances.

Antigen: A substance, usually a protein rather than carbohydrate or fat, which is foreign to the body and triggers a reaction that destroys or eliminates that substance. Antigens may be living things such as bacteria and molds or products of living things such as poisons, animal hairs, pollens or foods.

Autoimmune disease: A disease in which the immune system attacks and damages the body's own cells, tissues or organs. Diabetes, multiple sclerosis and rheumatoid arthritis are examples of autoimmune diseases.

Biopsy: A procedure involving the removal of living tissue to examine it under microscope for the purpose of diagnosing disease.

Candida albicans: Yeast capable of provoking a multitude of symptoms when it is present in the body in an excessive quantity.

Cell: The smallest unit of a living organism; the basic structure for tissues and organs.

Congenital: Present at birth.

DNA: Also called deoxyribonucleic acid, it represents the genetic blueprint in cells essential for protein synthesis, cellular reproduction and hereditary transfer.

Gliadin: A protein found in wheat gluten. In people with celiac disease, gliadin and similar proteins in rye, oats and barley work as antigens. The body reacts against these antigens, damaging the inside lining of the intestine.

Gluten: A generic term for the water-insoluble proteins found in all cereal grains. Gluten is found in wheat, rye, oats and barley, and is known to damage the intestine of those with celiac disease.

Immune system: It is an exceedingly complex system of specialized cells that defends the body from infectious disease-causing organisms.

Lymphoma: A variety of cancer characterized by the uncontrollable multiplication of lymph cells. People with celiac disease are 40 to 100 times more likely to develop intestinal lymphoma than those unaffected.

Malabsorption: Failure of the intestine to break down food and get it into the body. It causes food to be lost into stools, usually resulting in diarrhea.

Mucosa: The inside lining of the intestinal tract that absorbs food into the body.

Myelin: A substance constituted of fatty material and proteins that form a thick sheath around certain nerves.

Neurotransmitter: Chemicals that transmit messages between nerve cells in the form of nerve impulses. They affect physical and behavioral processes such as learning, memory, mood, sleep and response to pain.

Nutriment: All elements contained in foods and that can be assimilated by body cells. They are usually classified into carbohydrates, fats, vitamins and mineral salts.

Osteomalacia: Osteomalacia means softening of the bones. This softening occurs from a loss of the mineral calcium from the skeleton; the bones become flexible and gradually are molded by forces, such as bearing weight, that are exerted on them. Deformities can then result. When osteomalacia occurs in children, it is termed rickets. One of the two most common causes of osteomalacia is a problem of fat malabsorption called steatorrhea. In this condition, the body is unable to absorb fats, and they are passed directly out of the body in the stool. The result of this problem is that vitamin D, which is usually absorbed with fat, and calcium are poorly absorbed. This poor absorption can be a result of digestive disorders.

RNA: Also called ribonucleic acid. A substance found in plant and animal cells that carries genetic instructions from DNA. Important in the production of proteins.

Small intestine: Extending from the stomach to the large intestine, the small intestine is composed of three sections: duodenum, jejunum and ileum. It is involved in the absorption of nutrients and is affected by celiac disease.

Steatorrhea: A condition characterized by foul, frothy, sometimes floating stools, in which there is an abnormally large amount of fat in the stool. It is usually the result of poor absorption in the small intestine.

Tissue: Four major kinds of tissue make up the human body: epithelial, muscle, connective and nervous. Each type of tissue has unique characteristics that enable the tissue to perform its particular function.

Villus (plural–villi): The finger-like pattern of intestinal mucosa that is required for food absorption.

Villus atrophy: Damage or inflammation to the intestinal mucosa in which the finger-like projections called villi are "shaved-off". Villus atrophy occurs in people with celiac disease when they consume foods containing gluten.

Notes

Chapter 1

1 Dr. James S. Steward, consultant physician, History of the Coeliac condition, http://osiris.sunderland.ac.uk, p. 1

2 Beatrice Trum Hunter, Gluten intolerance, Keat Publishing, 1987, p. 3

3 Idem (1)

4 Danna Korn, Kids with celiac disease Woodbine House, 2001, p. xix

5 Dr. James S. Steward, consultant physician, History of the Coeliac condition, http://osiris.sunderland.ac.uk, p. 1

6Association canadienne de la maladie coeliaque, www.celiac.ca

Chapter 2

1 Sprue-Nik Press Eighteenth Edition, March 1995, "Celiac in the 90's"

2 J Pediatri Gastroenterol Nutr, 1995 July,21:1, 69-72

3 Scand J, Gastroenterol, 1995 Nov, 30:11, 1077-81(Ciacci et al)

Chapter 3

1 Sprue-Nik Press Eighteenth Edition, March 1995, "Celiac in the 90's"

Chapter 4

1 P. Marie, L. Miravet. Ostéomalacies, in Maladies métaboliques osseuses de l'adulte- D. Kuntz ed. Medecine Sciences Flammarion, Paris, 1996, pp 218-233

2 Dr. Joseph Mercola, Optimal Wellness Health News, March 5, 2000, Issue #143

3Hallert C, Astrom J, Walan A. Reversal of psychopathology in adult celiac disease with the aid of pyridoxine (vitamin B6). Scand J Gastroenterol 1983;18:299-304

4 Corvaglia L, Catamo R, Pepe G, Lazzari R, Corvaglia E, Depression in adult untreated celiac subjects: diagnosis by a pediatrician, American Journal of Gastroenterology: 1999, Mar; 94(3): 839-43

5 Saelid G, et al. "Peptide-containing fractions in depression", Biol Psychiatry 1985;20: 245-256

6 New York Times, Sept.13, 1994, genetics stydy by Dr. John Todd at Oxford

7 J Pediatr Gastroenterol Nutr 2001;33:462-465

8 American Journal of Medical Genetics, 2001;98:70-74

9 Beatrice Trum Hunter, Gluten Intolerance, Keats Publishing Inc, p 10

10 Gluten Intolerance, Beatrice Trim Hunter, Keats Publishing 1987, page 10-11

11 http;//www.nutramed.com/digestion/gluten.htm

12 Scott DL, Coulton BL, Symmons DPM, et al.: Long-term outcome of treating rheumatoid arthritis: Results after 20 years. Lancet i:1108-11, 1989

13 Carl C. Pfeiffer, PH.D, M.D., Nutrition and mental illness, p. 53

14 Beatrice Trum Hunter, Gluten intolerance, p 12-13

15 Dr. Dohan, F. C., More on celiac disease as a model for schizophrenia, 1983 Biol. Psychiatry 18:561-4

16 J Intern Med 1997 Nov;242(5):421-3

17 Gut 2000; 46: 332-335

18 Ciacci c, Cirillo M, Auriemma G, Di Dato G, Sabbatini F, Mazzacca G.,
Am J Gastroenterol, 1996; 91 (4): 718-22

19 Lancet 2000;356:399-400

Chapter 5

1 GUT 2002;50:332-5

2 Zoltan P. Rona, Return to the joy of health, 1995, p. 328

3 Auricchio S et al. Does breastfeeding protect against the development of clinical symptoms of celiac disease in children, J Pediatr Gastroenterol Nutr 1983; 2 (3) :428-33

4 Auriccio, 1983 ; Greco et al.,1988 ; Kelly, 1989

5 Bourguerra F et al., Breastfeeding effect relative to age of onset of celiac disease, Arch Pediatr, 1998, Jun :5(6) :621-6
6 Article from Karoly Horvath, M.D., www.celiac.com
7 Troncone R. et al, Passage of gliadin into human breast milk, Acta Pediatr Scand, 76 :453, 1987

Chapter 6
1 The Canandian Celiac Associaltion Handbook, 3e édition, p53
2 Ann Whealan, Gluten-Free Living de Septembre/Octobre, 2000
3 Gluten-Free Living Magazine, Mars/Avril 1999
4 "Products for patients with special needs," Non-prescription products: Formulations and Features, 97-98, pp.14-17, American Pharmaceuticals Association

Chapter 7
1 Kids with celiac disease, Danna Korn, 2001, p.125

Conclusion
1 Lancet 2000, 29 avril; 355: 1518-9
2 Lancet 2002, 16 mars; 359: 945-946

Bibliography

Atlas du corps humain et de la sexualité, Éditions Sans Frontière, 1989.

Baggish, Jeff, How your immune system works, Ziff-Davis Press, 1994.

Balch, James, F. and Balch Phyllis, A., Prescription for nutritional healing, Avery Publishing Group Inc., 1990.

Barczak, Carola, How to manage common food allergies and retain your sanity, Health Naturally, June/July 1998.

Bateson-Koch, Carolee, Allergies, disease in disguise, Alive Books, 1994.

Bennett, Aileen, M., Coping with celiac, the great masquerader, A + G Publishing, 1998.

Bland, Jeffrey, S., Applying new essentials in nutritional medicine, HealthComm International Inc., 1995

Brunner Sholtis, Lillian and Suddarth Smith, Doris, Soins infirmiers en médecine-chirurgie, Éditions du Renouveau Pédagogique Inc., 1985.

Chaput, Mario, Traitement naturel des allergies, Fleurs sociales, 2000.

Comby, Bruno, Renforcez votre immunité, Les éditions de l'homme, 1994.

Courchesne, Dr. Alain, L'énergie douce des thérapies naturelles, Éditions de Mortagne, 1993.

Crook, William, G. and Hurt Jones, Marjorie, The yeast connection cookbook, Professional Books, 1989.

Davies, Lesley, Grains from your health food store, Alive Canadian Journal of health and nutrition, October, 1991.

Elie, Monick Juliette, Un blé noir porteur de lumière : le sarrasin, Vitalité Québec, March 2002.

Erasmus, Udo, Essential fat facts, Alive Canadian Journal of health and nutrition, November 1999

Fattorusso, V, and Ritter, O., Vademecum Clinique (15th edition), Masson, 1998.

Frenette, Gisèle, Séance de nutrition (document), 1995.

Garrison, Robert, Jr., and Somer, Elizabeth, The nutrition desk reference, Keats Publishing Inc., Connecticut, 1985.

Howell, Dr Edward, Enzyme nutrition, the food enzyme concept, Avery Publishing Group Inc., 1985.

Hurt Jones, Marjorie, Super Foods, Mast Enterprises Inc., 1990.

Keith, Velma J., and Gordon, Monteen, The how to herb book, Mayfield Publications, 1984.

Korn Danna, Kids with celiac disease, Woodbine House, 2000.

Kousmine, Dr. C., Soyez bien dans votre assiette jusqu'à 80 ans et plus, Primeur/Sand, 1985.

L'Académie de phytothérapie du Québec, Inc, Nutrition et vitamino-thérapie, Les Laboratoires Vachon, Inc.

La pharmacie naturelle, L'immunité, détails inconnus.

Laberge, Danièle, Les allergies alimentaires, Armoire aux herbes, inc.

Lee, John, R., What your doctor may not tell you about menopause, Warner Books, 1996.

Le Fers-Dupac, Pénélope, 230 recettes spéciales pour allergies au gluten, Jacques Grancher, 1982.

Lipski, Elizabeth, Leaky gut syndrome, Keats Publishing, Los Angeles, 1998.

Marieb, Elaine N., and Laurendeau, Guy, Anatomie et physiologie humaines, Éditions du Renouveau pédagogique Inc., 1993.

Matsen, Dr John, Eating Alive, Crompton Books, 1987.

Mindell, Earl, Vitamin Bible, Warner Books, 1991.

Murray, Michael, T., Arthritis, Prima Publishing, 1994.

Pfeiffer, Carl, C., Nutrition and mental illness, Healing Arts Press, 1987.

Riordan, J., and Auerbach, K., Breasfeeding and human lactation (2e édition), Boston and London: Jones and Bartlett, 1999.

Rona, Zoltan, Encyclopedia of Natural Healing, Alive Publishing Inc., 1997.

Rona, Zoltan, Return to the joy of health, Alive Books, 1995.

Rudin, Donald and Felix, Clara, Omega 3 oils, Avery Publishing Group, 1996.

Starenkyj, Danièle, Le mal du sucre, Publications Orion Inc., 10th edition, 1990.

Taber's cyclopedic medical dictionary (10e edition), The Ryerson Press, 1965.

Trum Hunter, Beatrice, Gluten intolerance, Keats Publishing Inc., Los Angeles, 1987.

Werbach, Melvyn, R, Nutritional influences on illness (2nd edition), Third Line Press, 1993.

Printed in Great Britain
by Amazon